DECODED MONEY

THE SECRETS OF HOW TO GET RID OFF FINANCIAL WORRIES/ INSECURITIES AND ACHIEVE PEACE OF MIND WITH MONEY

BRIJESH PARIKH,CWM

Contents

Contents

Contents

Contents

About The Author

My Mission to help 100000 Families to Live a financially Worry-Free Life and Achieve Financial Freedom...

I have been an avid learner of personal finance since 2002 when I procured reading material of Post Graduate Diploma in Financial Advising by Indian Institute of Banking and Finance in collaboration with Australian Securities Institute.

In fact, regular Savings and Investments habits were inherited in me from my mother and father. At that point in time our investments into reliance shares helped our family to do major expenses such as Marriages.

I studied Personal Finance for managing my own personal finance well. I was interested to start consulting for personal finance during 2002-3 but it was time dominated by Agents and Distributors who were buying customers by sharing a hefty portion of commissions they earn to customers under the table, which I didn't wanted to do. So, time was not right for starting fee based financial advisory practice. So, I continued my Education and Training Business as an Edupreneur.

In 2013 SEBI came up with SEBI Investments Advisor Regulations 2013 to pave way for Fiduciary (Putting clients Interest Ahead of Advisor Interest) Advisory Practice and I though time has come for me to review my decision to start Advisory Practice. I took Licence and Started Helping Individuals and Families to Manage Their Finances better and create wealth.

While I was working to start my practice, my friends working in Personal Finance Industry discouraged me to not to start Fees only advisory as according to them, investor still seek some money as rebate from agent's commission even while investing in liquid funds.

My intention to start a fiduciary practice didn't deter by such discouraging feedback. I started Practicing and got good response but in City Like Bhavnagar, I realised that its going to take years to create awareness and reach masses.

So, i have now decided to use digital medium to reach 100000 families by way of offering 'Do It Yourself (DIY) tutorial courses/material to help learn personal finance and wealth creation combining my Training Experience, Personal Finance and Wealth Creation Experience and Training.

I am writing this note to announce my initiative of Launching an online programme that will teach interested individuals to start their step-by-step journey of wealth creation, my programmme will focus on;

Knowledge of Managing Personal Finance

Having Right Kind of Mindset

A step-by-Step Tutorials to set up wealth creation System

Coaching and Mentoring by Creating Inner Circle and Regular Support Webinars and many more Sessions...

Please download all the resources discussed in this book from here :

https://links.planetwealth.in/decodedmoneyresources

I conducted a brief survey about what investor would like to learn and sharing my findings;

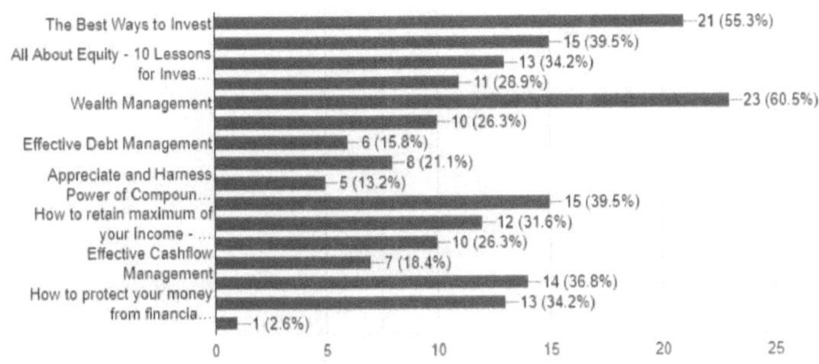

If you wish to be part of this empowerment initiative, pls join our group by clicking https://www.facebook.com/groups/1690622834523958/?ref=bookmarks....
Happy Financial Well-being , god bless....

WEALTH PRINCIPLES

PRINCIPLE-1

Understanding Power of Compounding

Power of compounding is 8th Wonder of the world. Those who understand it earn it and those who do not understand pays it. - Albert Einstein

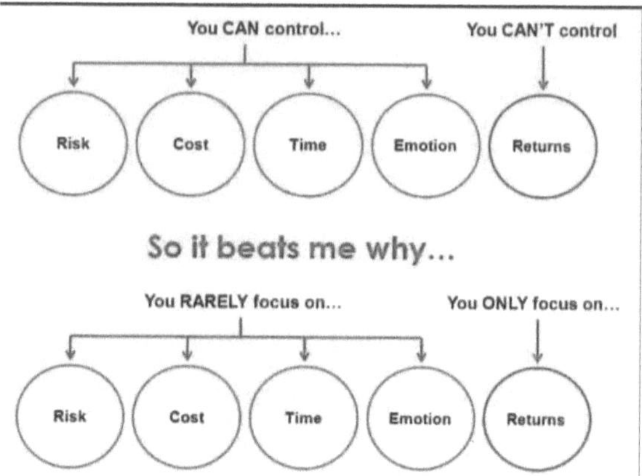

We all have learnt about compounding in our school maths. In its simplest term, its interest earned are added back to capital and again earning fresh interest on the enhanced capital or interest on interest.

This essential means if you keep your money remain invested for long-term compounding can do wonder for your money to grow.

Let's try to understand using an example.

Mr. A understands compounding and hence started investing Rs. 1000 at 28 years and continued to invest till the age of retirement, which is 58 years.
He invested Rs. 3.6 lakh.

Mr. B, who does not understand the power of compounding like Mr, A and started investing Rs. 1500 at 38 years , he is investing 50% more than Mr. A to cover time lost, and continued to invest till the age of 58 years.
He also invested Rs. 3.6 lakh.

Both have assumed to earn a compounded Annual Growth Rate of 10%.

Now who, according to you, would have accumulated what amount?

Mr. A could accumulate approx. 21 Lakh and Mr. B could hardly accumulate Rs. 11 Lakh almost 50% less than Mr. A despite of investing 50% more than Mr. A to cover lost years.

Compounding affects adversely purchasing power of your money against inflation as well. Value or purchasing power of Rs. 1 lakh in year 2018 would be Rs. 5402 in the year 2058 if inflation remains 8% throughout this period.

If you understand the power of compounding and generate positive real returns after tax and inflation, you can make your hard earned money work hard for you and if you do not understand inflation will reduce purchasing power of your money and you will pay for not understanding power of compounding.

So always ensure that your portfolios real return (returns after tax and i your inflation) are not negative and if you are conservative, it should be at least "0" and if you are Moderately aggressive, it could be 1 or 2% and if you are aggressive, it could be 4 to 5%.

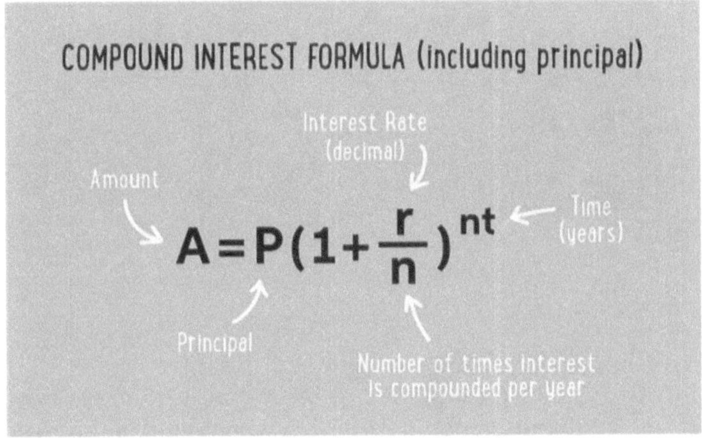

PRINCIPLE-2

How to manage cash flow by creating a budget - for beginners

Are you a Saver or a Spender or a Investor?

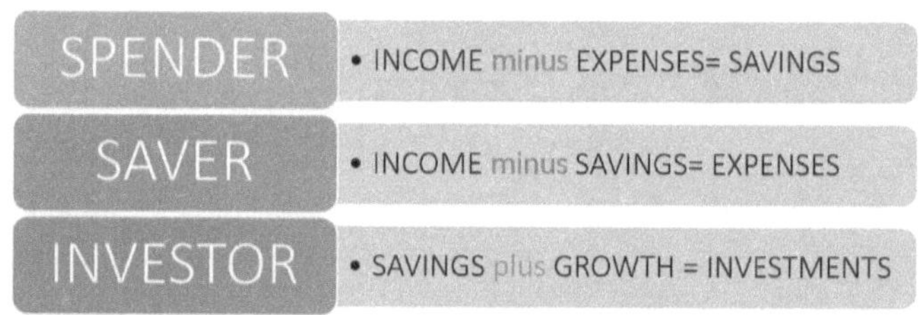

What is the budget for personal finance?

A budget is an estimation of income and expenses over a specified future period and is usually compiled and re-evaluated periodically. - Investopedia

It helps you to make right decisions about spending and saving your money -It enables you to avoid any unnecessary expenses. It helps you to plan your future financial needs.

Budgeting means controlling how you spend your money.

Money and water share same nature. If you do not provide direction to them, they will find their own direction, which may not be the direction as per your life priority.

- It helps you to avoid unnecessary purchases
- It helps you to save money on emergency expenses
- It helps you to plan for your future

What are the types of budgeting?

- Monthly Budget–This includes your fixed monthly expenditure like rent, electricity, telephone bill etc.
- Weekly Budget–This includes your weekly expenditure like grocery shopping, laundry, and utility bills.

Why you should create a budget?

Practicing budgeting in personal finance has several benefits, which include but are not limited to;

- it gives you a realistic view of what you can afford to spend, and what you should spend money on.
- It is important for every individual to have a budget, even if it's just a general idea of how much you are spending each month.
- It gives you a chance to make savings, which can pay off debts or invest in the future.
- It helps you to avoid unnecessary expenses that you may not need.
- It helps you to keep track of what you spend and saves money from being wasted.
- A budget is an essential tool for saving money, and also for spending wisely.

How to create your budget?

In order to create your budget you need to follow following steps either on a paper or in a spreadsheet software.

Step-1: List and record all your sources of income, such as salary, divided, business income, or pension. If you're a non-salaried earner, please find an average earning of your last 2-3 year's earnings or more years if recent years are more volatile.

Step-2: List and record all your regular expenses such as grocery, electricity, telephone, rent, EMIs, Internet, School Fees, Transportation, Fuel and likes.To assist you with this step, take out your checkbook or your most recent bank statement.

Step-3: List and record all your variable expenses, such as Yearly Insurance Premium, AMCs, etc.

Step-4: Subtract all your expenses (Regular and variable combined) from all your income and arrive at surplus.

If your surplus is positive, congrats you are living with your means. If your surplus is negative, which means you are spending more than your earnings and you are living a debt laden life and you need to give a hard look to your budget and find areas of cost cutting to create a positive surplus budget.

What care to take while creating your budget?

To make the numbers work, you must lower your spending and eliminate unnecessary purchases. This part isn't usually as enjoyable. In many budgets, the savings category gets whatever is left over after the more urgent expenses, and in most cases, the not so urgent ones as well have been paid.

Giving your savings the same priority as your living expenditures is the only way to take it seriously.

- **Wrong Formula: Income-Expense=Savings**
- **Right Formula: Income-Savings = Expense**

If you set aside a certain amount at the start of each month, your savings will increase considerably faster and you won't be able to unintentionally burn through cash on something else, and we understand saving might be difficult and that's if we even remember to do it at all. Savings automation is a simple method to keep track of your budget. To create your emergency fund. Set up automatic transfers from your checking account to your savings account to build your nest egg, open an individual retirement account and set up automatic deposits every pay day.

Don't be scared to experiment with several budgets until you find the one that works best for you or a combination of methods. Your budget doesn't have to be flawless. It simply needs to be appropriate for you. Be self-aware. You know how you're constantly being told to know yourself well. That doesn't just apply to your spiritual journey. It does to budgeting, too.

When you should create your budget?
You can create your budget anytime you like and then stick to it.

You should plan your budget during the time of financial stability.

Best time to put budgeting into practice is from your first salary/earning, as this will help you become for disciplined in managing your money effectively from day-1.

Who should create their own budget?
Everyone who is earning and responsible to manage finances of their family should create a budget.

PRINCIPLE-3

Financial Vision and Goals Articulation

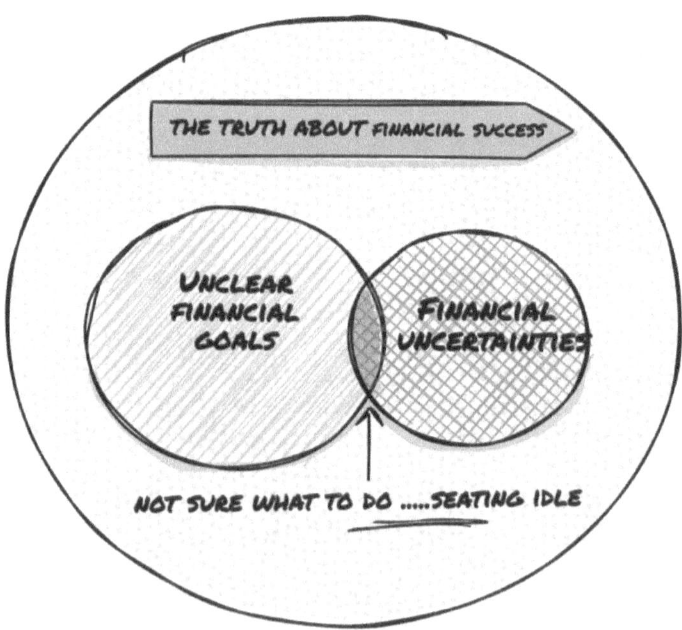

If you start your journey without deciding your destination, where will you reach? Probably nowhere, or at least not where you want to reach.

The same principle applies to personal finance. If you invest without deciding your financial vision and financial goals, you will probably accumulate some money, but surely not as much as you need to fund your financial goals and future.

Another principle about money is, Like water, it finds its own way if you do not provide a way to your money.

So it's essential for your financial well being to articulate a clear vision and goals about your financial future to ensure that you not only achieve your financial goals and future but do not miss any wealth creation opportunity that is there in your personal finance.

Let me share one example, one of my client share he felt it comfortable to start an SIP of Rs. 40,000 per month and after his financial goals articulation and budgeting exercise, we could find that his monthly surplus is around Rs. 85,000 so we invested Rs. 70,000 per month which is almost 80% more than what he was comfortable before financial goals and vision articulation.

Now you can understand and appreciate role of having financial vision and goals in your wealth creation.

Now the question comes: why people do not create financial vision and set financial goals? Basically majority of people struggle with thinking about future and that too for financial goals. They found it very daunting, so they keep on avoiding thinking about the same.

I have observed, during working with 100s of clients, that if you work with a professional financial planner for your financial plan, he will help you articulate your financial vision and financial goals in a much better way so that you have much better clarity about your financial priorities and can manage your cash flow according to your financial vision and to achieve your financial priorities.

PRINCIPLE-4

Effective Debt Management

There are 3 pillars of wealth creation: first one is effective Cashflow management to create required investible surplus, second one is generating positive real returns (Return-Taxes-Inflation) and third one is managing debt effectively.

The first two pillars I have discussed elsewhere, let's discuss effective debt management. There are two types of debts; 1) Good Debt and 2) Bad debt.

Good Debt: is debt that generates assets that appreciate. For Example - Housing Loan, Education Loan, Business Loan.

Bad Debt: is debt that is used to gain depreciating assets. For Example - Car Loan, Credit Card Loan.

One must consider cost of loan vs. returns generated from the assets gained through the loan and if cost of loan is less than returns generated, than and then only loan is to be taken. You must also check your cash-flow situation while taking a loan from the perspective of EMI. Your EMIs would be monthly and you should be able to fund your needs and investments for your future financial goals after paying EMIs, and if that is not the situation, you should not take that loan.

If you are already having debt burden, let me share few ways to be debt free early.

5 Ways to Pay Off Your Loan Early

With the right mindset and a commitment to pay it off, you can pay off the Loan early.

It can save you Lakhs of Rupees in the long run if you decide to make that commitment. Look at this example:

You borrowed for Rs. 1500000 home with a 20-year term Loan at 8% interest. By the end of 20 years, you'll have almost doubled the amount you spend because you'll pay over Rupees 1511000 in interest!

Thinking of how much you'll owe in interest may make you a little sick to your stomach, so let's look at the ways you might nip your loan in the bud early.

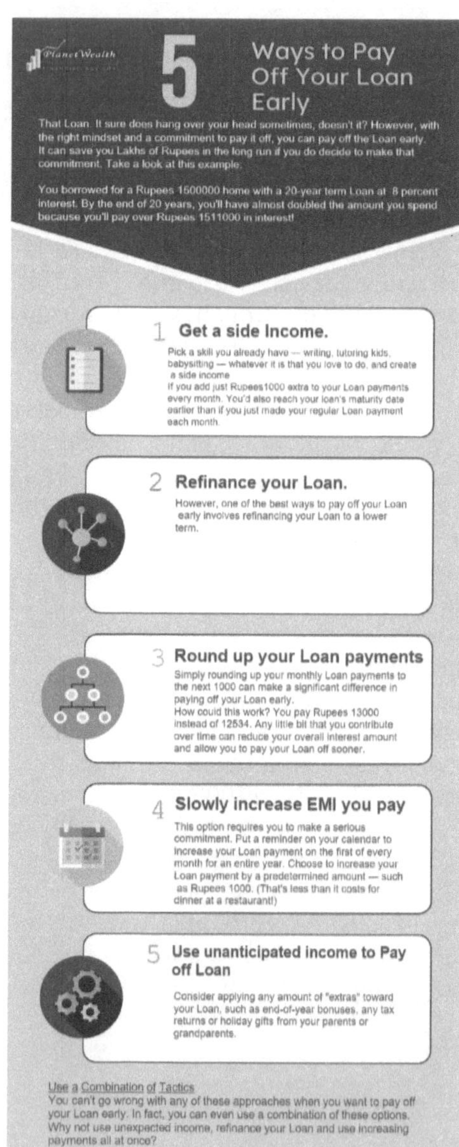

PlanetWealth

5 Ways to Pay Off Your Loan Early

That Loan. It sure does hang over your head sometimes, doesn't it? However, with the right mindset and a commitment to pay it off, you can pay off the Loan early. It can save you Lakhs of Rupees in the long run if you do decide to make that commitment. Take a look at this example.

You borrowed for a Rupees 1500000 home with a 20-year term Loan at 8 percent interest. By the end of 20 years, you'll have almost doubled the amount you spend because you'll pay over Rupees 1511000 in interest!

1 Get a side Income.
Pick a skill you already have — writing, tutoring kids, babysitting — whatever it is that you love to do, and create a side income
If you add just Rupees1000 extra to your Loan payments every month. You'd also reach your loan's maturity date earlier than if you just made your regular Loan payment each month.

2 Refinance your Loan.
However, one of the best ways to pay off your Loan early involves refinancing your Loan to a lower term.

3 Round up your Loan payments
Simply rounding up your monthly Loan payments to the next 1000 can make a significant difference in paying off your Loan early.
How could this work? You pay Rupees 13000 instead of 12534. Any little bit that you contribute over time can reduce your overall interest amount and allow you to pay your Loan off sooner.

4 Slowly increase EMI you pay
This option requires you to make a serious commitment. Put a reminder on your calendar to increase your Loan payment on the first of every month for an entire year. Choose to increase your Loan payment by a predetermined amount — such as Rupees 1000. (That's less than it costs for dinner at a restaurant!)

5 Use unanticipated income to Pay off Loan
Consider applying any amount of "extras" toward your Loan, such as end-of-year bonuses, any tax returns or holiday gifts from your parents or grandparents.

Use a Combination of Tactics
You can't go wrong with any of these approaches when you want to pay off your Loan early. In fact, you can even use a combination of these options. Why not use unexpected income, refinance your Loan and use increasing payments all at once?

1. Get a side income.
You may need to come up with extra money to make extra loan payments, so why not consider a side income?

Pick a skill you already have — writing, tutoring kids, babysitting — whatever you love to do, and create a side income.

If you add just Rupees1000 extra to your loan payments every month. You'd also reach your loan's maturity date earlier than if you just made your regular loan payment each month.

2. Refinance your loan.
Refinancing your loan simply means that you opt for either a lower interest rate or shorter term on your loan — or both. You can also get cash out of your home's equity when you refinance.

However, one of the best ways to pay off your loan early involves refinancing your loan to a lower term. For example, you may choose to refinance from a 20-year Loan to a 15-year Loan.

For example, let's say that you bought Rs.1500000 home at an 8% interest rate with a 20-year term. You'd pay Rupees 12547 monthly and over the course of 20 years, the home would cost you Rs. 3011000 (if you made no down payment at all).

Let's say you chose a 15-year loan at 7% interest rate. You'd pay Rs. 13482 per month and would cost you Rs.2426000 total over the course of 15 years (without a down payment).

You'll own your home faster and save a lot of money when you switch to a 15-year loan. As you can see, 15-year loans have lower interest rates but carry higher monthly payments.

3. Round up your loan payments.
Not interested in refinancing or making biweekly payments? Simply rounding up your monthly loan payments to the next 1000 can make a significant

difference in paying off your loan early.

How could this work? You pay Rupees 13000 instead of 12534. Any little that you contribute over time can reduce your overall interest amount and allow you to pay your loan off sooner.

4. *Slowly increase the amount you pay.*

This option requires you to make a serious commitment. Put a reminder on your calendar to increase your loan payment on the first of every month for an entire year. Choose to increase your loan payment by a predetermined amount — such as Rs. 1000. (That's less than it costs for dinner at a restaurant!)

By slowly raising the amount you pay, you'll never notice a difference.

5. *Apply unanticipated income toward the Loan.*

Did Great Aunt leave you money when she passed? Instead of splurging on a hot tub, use that unexpected gift to make an extra loan payment. Even though it really doesn't seem like fun to use a windfall this way, it might make the most sense if you want to pay off your loan early.

Make a list of other ways you might use extra income to apply it to your loan. Consider applying any amount of "extras" toward your loan, such as end-of-year bonuses, any tax returns or holiday gifts from your parents or grandparents.

Use a Combination of Tactics

You can't go wrong with any of these approaches when you want to pay off your loan early. In fact, you can even use a combination of these options. Why not use unexpected income, refinance your loan and use biweekly payments all at once?

Attacking your loan from several angles can help you meet your goals in no time at all. You might even end up paying your loan off way sooner than you expected because you build momentum toward paying off your loan!

PRINCIPLE-5

Understanding Real Returns

There are 3 Pillars of wealth creation, first one is to create new capital for investments by managing cash flow effectively that balances between present and future, second one is to grow your hard earned money and the third one is manage your loans/debt efficiently.

Let's understand how to grow your hard earned money. Before we discuss how you can grow your hard earned money, let's first understand what are enemies of your investment returns.

First Enemy is tax. It's said that there are only two certain things in the life tax and death.

Second enemy is inflation. Inflation eats away purchasing power of your corpus. The issue with inflation is that it is not visible in the short time period, so you do not realize its impact. If your investment returns are not equal or greater than your inflation, you will fall short of corpus required to fund your financial goals.

So, while managing your investments, your risk optimized real returns should be positive. Which means your returns from your investment portfolio should be positive after providing for Taxes and Inflation. You need to consider your lifestyle inflation and not government inflation.

Real Returns = (returns from Portfolio - Taxes. If any - your life style inflation)

It is imperative for investors to understand and appreciate real returns and not to have negative real returns but at least have 0 real returns (if your risk profile is extremely conservative) or better have positive real returns (how much is determined by your risk profile).

CREATING WEALTH MINDSET

PROCRASTINATION VS. WEALTH: HOW IT CAN AFFECT YOUR FINANCIAL SUCCESS

Procrastinating is postponing the performance of tasks. It may seem normal, but procrastination is an enemy of wealth and can affect your financial success.

In this article, I will show you the relationship between procrastination and wealth and how to fight it to achieve financial success.

Why do some people like to procrastinate?

According to experts, the act of procrastinating is linked to immediate pleasures. We are willing to feel immediate pleasure, even if this activity impedes the future.

Therefore, many people feel good procrastinating, as they invest their time in activities that bring joy and postpone painful or laborious activities.

Other people are comfortable procrastinating because they are used to working under pressure.

It is important to have self-knowledge in this quest for greater productivity in search of wealth.

Check out some ways how procrastination may prevent your wealth:

Poor time management

One way that procrastination has to keep you away from wealth is by disrupting your way of dealing with time.

Procrastination causes you to have poor time management and you deliver your tasks at the last minute and end up hurting yourself.

Negative habits

Procrastinating creates negative habits that can harm your future. With your finances, you tend to be disorganized, having the habit of spending without worrying about the future, because a procrastinator is never focused on what can happen, but on what is happening.

Low productivity

Acquiring negative habits, delivering projects at the last minute, postponing tasks and missing deadlines is a way to contribute to lower your productivity.

Having low productivity goes against wealth plans. After all, you cannot solve everything you need and you will not have a good professional return.

Lack of organization

The procrastinator is usually a disorganized person, which generates indiscipline, you end up creating a greater disorganization, not being able to control your activities.

Deferring payments

Procrastinators tend to postpone everything, including payments. They avoid paying bills in advance, leaving it until the last minute, as they do not have a financial plan and end up dropping it, increasing the interest and fines on the bills.

Not an investor

A procrastinator will never be an investor. You will never have your money invested and growing.

This is because the procrastinator does not think about the future, cannot make plans, setting goals. He always seeks to skip steps, reducing his work.

These are some of the ways that procrastination can become the chief enemy of wealth.

How to end procrastination

But now that you know how procrastination can harm you financially, how about learning how to fight it?

Find out how to stop procrastination once and for all

Where does procrastination come from?

The first step is to understand where your procrastination comes from, where it came from and what triggers procrastinating behaviors.

Notice in which situations you procrastinate the most, which of these situations you feel most comfortable postponing tasks.

Also, note what your havens are when you are procrastinating, what activities you do when you are putting off important tasks.

What is the reason for procrastination? Laziness? Tiredness? Pressure? Fear? It is important to identify what are the main reasons you procrastinate.

This way, you can understand the problem at its root and focus on solving it more effectively.

How to Overcome Procrastination:

- **Set goals**

Having defined goals and objectives is very important for you to become a productive person and leave procrastination behind.

Having a goal in mind is what will move all of your actions. Therefore, it is essential to have this aim.

- **Have small goals**

It is important to divide the main aim or goal into small goals. This is because you will be able to better manage these goals and will remain more disciplined.

In addition, you will be closely monitoring your evolution in reaching your goal.

- **Increase your productivity**

Use some methods to increase your productivity during the day. Use methods like Pomodoro, Ivy Lee or Matrix Eisenhower to organize your priorities.

This way, you can increase your productivity without wasting a lot of time on less important tasks.

- **Plan your day**

Plan your day the night before. List everything you need to do and determine the deadlines for each activity.

These are ways to avoid procrastination and stick to your bigger goal.

Procrastinating can damage your professional and financial plans, besides damaging your emotionally.

DISASTROUS ROLE OF SOCIAL PROOF - HERD'S MENTALITY IN INVESTING

H ave you ever clapped as others are clapping without knowing for what it is being clapped?

Have you ever laughed at a joke as others are laughing whereas you could not understand the joke?

If yes, well, you have also showed herd mentality.

We all, at some or other point in time in life, become a victim of this emotional or behavioural bias.

Today we are going to discuss how herd mentality can be disastrous in investments

Let's take the recent example of Zomato IPO. A company making losses with no history of Profit offers shares of Rs. 10 Face value at Rs. 76 which is almost 7.5 times of face value is subscribed 38.5 times and gets listed at Rs. 116 almost > 50% Listing gains.

Let's revisit common investing wisdom; The company we are looking to invest in should have demonstrated profitability and should have visibility of good financial performance in the future are two major criteria apart from other valuations metrics.

If we look at Zomato, it has no history of profitability and then also investors rushed to pay 7.5 times what the promoter paid. Whether it will be profitable in the future is yet to be seen.

This is a classic example of herd mentality winning over common investing wisdom.

Now there will be two outcomes for those who invested on listing day: either they will have to wait years for their shares to be appreciated as and when the company turns profitable or if it didn't, they will lose their money.

There are plenty of companies in the market at the time of Zomato IPO available with a strong history of profitability, strong financial future, and fair valuations for investors to invest and gain benefit out of investing in such companies.

Just how evil is social proof? Consider the following example: Many investors believe that a sure thing is to invest in something "everyone" is investing in. For example, if everyone is buying Zomato, then you can be sure it will continue to rise in price!

Social proof, at least from a rational point of view, is almost always extremely overrated. Almost always. There is a very rare situation when it is a useful tool for evaluating a purchase choice.

And, as we'll soon see, there is one situation where it is a killer. Namely: When it comes to deciding about our personal relationships. The "Curse of Knowledge" Listen up: One of the major reasons people don't go ahead and do something they've been putting off is... they are waiting for "proof." In other words, they want some outside influence to make them "feel" good about taking that first step. Like, "Oh yeah? Well, I don't feel good about this, so you must be wrong."

Know this: If you tell someone something they already know (their own feelings) they will often not change their mind.

Examples of Social Proof Bias

1. Investors in a crisis, for example, during a bear market phase, would like to follow the herd and decide accordingly. If many people are selling, they will also sell their holdings, even if booking losses.

2. Giving a Like status for a message in social media networks, just because our friends have given a Like.

3. Checking online for reviews and deciding on the restaurant which has got the most positive reviews.

4. Following the experts' advice or peers' decisions in investing.

5. Can you stick to your portfolio when everyone else claims the market is about to go into a recession?

Overcoming Social proof bias

1. Filter the news and information and take only the ones that are necessary

2. Ignore the big hue and cry or joy and greed, and look at things objectively, keeping emotions aside.

3. Ask yourself if the decision you are about to make is only after proper analysis, or are you are just following someone else?

Hope after reading to this, you will save yourself from mistakes due Herd Mentality behaviour in general and in investing particularly.

Investing Risk - It's Never a Choice Between Risk or No-Risk, But Risk Now or Later

Risk comes from not knowing what you are doing. - Warren Buffett.

If you know what you are doing and risks involved, you have a better chance of getting success.

During my career as Wealth coach, I have seen many investors making the mistake of either chasing the return or shying away from taking risk. But let me tell you that you do not have a choice of taking a risk or not, but you have a choice of taking risk now or later?

There are many risks involved in investing, but the most important risk and investor need to worry about is not having the required corpus for the financial goal for which you have been saving and investing.

You are sacrificing in the present to improve your future while you are investing. And what is the point of sacrificing in the present when you can not accumulate adequate corpus for your financial future?

If you invest into so-called safe investments such as Government Securities or Bank Fixed Deposits, you are risking losing purchasing power of your money as your post tax returns would be less than inflation, which ultimately leads to an inadequate corpus for your future financial goals. So risk of not accumulating adequate corpus is also there, if you invest into so-called safe investments.

If you invest into growth asset class such as equity, you are risking losing your capital if equity market correct but if you have enough time to tide over correction and know some basic investing or hire a proper professional, you can accumulate enough corpus to fund your future financial goals.

So as, I said earlier it is never a choice of risk or no-risk but a choice of taking risk now by investing into equity and face volatility of markets to accumulate adequate corpus or avoid risk to future by investing into fixed safe securities like government securities and lose purchasing power of your money against inflation.

Please note I am neither favoring equity investing nor opposing investing into government securities. My point here is that you have to take risk if you wish to grow your money to achieve your financial goals. How much and what type of risk is always debatable based on your risk profile?

The best way is to take and manage risk by following asset allocation and periodic rebalancing.

Don't Lose Patience with Your Investments

"The stock market is a device to transfer money from the impatient to the patient." — Warren Buffett

Successful investors develop several valuable skills over their lifetimes. You're not born knowing how to research a stock or how to apply critical thinking to an investment opportunity — those are investing skills some people learn and develop. Patience is an important, but often under used, investment skill we believe many need to develop more fully. We're not born patient. When we're young, we care most about instant gratification. Just ask any parent who's had to deal with temper tantrums. But patience can be learned and, if you're an investor, learning it could help you reach your financial goals.

Why Patience Is So Important?
In today's world of 24/7 news cycles, constantly changing sentiments, moon boy shills, and record-high levels of uncertainty, you would be dishonest if you said you've never once felt lost, confused, or emotional.

At its worst, today's financial media encourages investors to take excess action, which is actually one of the worst things one can do in investing. The most important principle in investing is not how savvy your trading chops are, but something quite the opposite: patience.

Why Is it so Hard to Be Patient?

Simply put, your brain makes it hard to be patient. Human beings were designed to react to threats, either real or perceived. Stressful situations trigger a physiological response in people. You've likely heard this called the "fight-or-flight" response — either attack or run away, whatever helps ease the threat.

The problem is, your body doesn't recognize the difference between true physical danger (during which fighting or fleeing would actually be helpful) and psychological triggers, like scary movies. Being patient is difficult because it means overcoming these natural instincts. Turbulent financial markets can trigger the response too but, unlike scary movies, there can be real-world affects you'll need patience to overcome.

When markets are seesawing and you're overwhelmed with negative financial media, as we experienced this year during the pandemic-driven bear market, your brain perceives a threat to your financial well-being. Even though stock market volatility isn't a physical threat, the fight-or-flight response kicks in, emotion takes over, and your brain tells you to do something. Your investment portfolio is being harmed! Take action! Now! With investing, action too often translates into selling something because selling feels like you're shielding your portfolio from further harm. But selling at the wrong time — like in the middle of a major downturn — is one of the biggest investment mistakes you can make.

Key Benefits of Being Patient:

- **Tax benefits**: In almost all countries, the government rewards patience by having higher taxes on short-term capital gains as compared to long-term capital gains. Take advantage of it.
- **Reduces mistakes**: Natural bias of humans is to act. So when we hear an idea about buying a new stock or cryptocurrency, we are more worried about what would happen if we don't buy — we may miss a great opportunity (loss aversion bias). This causes investors to have too many assets in their portfolios. A few weeks/ months later, these same investors don't have the slightest inkling of why those assets were bought in the first place, and no idea what to do next with them.
- **Develops conviction**: A deep understanding of the token or company, its business model, and its ecosystem can help investors build strong convictions about the company. Ongoing diligence helps one understand how the company is reacting to various exogenous and endogenous events. With conviction, an investor can act decisively by either buying a meaningful chunk or leaving the asset alone. A strong conviction will allow an investor to hold on to a position when the market is in turmoil. However, building conviction requires patience and working through the tedious process that is investing.

Here are a few strategies you can use to cultivate patience and clarity of thought in your investing decisions:

Have a plan and think long term. Set long-term financial goals and keep them in front of mind during volatile times. A written financial plan is a great idea. Long-term thinking helps you mentally separate your investing journey from your long-term financial destination.

Keeping a long-term perspective will give you the psychological fortitude you need to grow your portfolio over the long term. If you have trouble thinking about the long term during volatile times, consider using a trusted financial professional to help keep you on track.

Understand that market volatility is normal. Just like lines at the grocery store checkout, market volatility is a normal part of life. It might still be unpleasant at the moment, but recognizing that you'll encounter volatile markets from time to time can help you mentally prepare yourself.

Remember, time is on your side. Take solace in the long history of capital markets. Corrections are temporary and usually brief and even bear markets eventually end. Historically, markets go up far more often and by a much greater margin than they go down. Owning assets for the long term, assuming they are high quality, and you didn't buy the peak, is one of the best ways to profit from economic progress, innovation, and compound growth.

Don't look at market prices too often: Looking at market prices often causes us to expend a lot of emotional energy on either elation or dejection. Warren Buffett's famous dictum should always be remembered, "The market is there to serve you, not instruct you."

Control Your Emotions. Buy Low, Sell High: Patience will be extremely hard to practice if you FOMO into the peak of a bull market, and plan to "hold it" for the next 2–3 year bear market. Once you've stopped yourself from making irrational investment decisions based on greed or fear, you'll find being patient much easier.

And finally, being patient isn't just something you do during bull markets. Patience can actually be rewarded much more during bear markets, where sometimes investors will decrease their position sizing, wait patiently, and start accumulating only after we've reached undervalued range.

Throwing Good Money after bad money–The Sunk Cost Fallacy

In economics and business decision-making, a sunk cost (also known as retrospective cost) is a cost that has already been incurred and cannot be recovered–Wikipedia

Examples of Sunk Cost Fallacy

1. How many of us have kept on spending money on fixing washing machines and other electrical/ electronic goods when they have problems? Most of us would have gone through this, even though the new equipment would have cost closer to same repair or annual maintenance charges, or even less? Same could be with 'my first car' sentiment and keep on spending money on its repairs.

2. A Term plan is the great insurance for life cover, but many of us have bought endowment and money back policies, which pay meagre 5% returns, but charge huge premiums. We also continue to pay premiums for these, just because we have paid few premiums already. They can consider surrendering the policy after 3 years or convert them to 'paid up' policies.

3. In a casino, we could have seen many people playing again and again to win somehow to recover the cost or amount that they have already spent and sunk. They think that if they don't win the prize; the money spent already in the game will have been wasted.

The sunk cost fallacy is most dangerous when we have invested a lot of time, money, energy and love in something. This investment becomes a reason to carry on, even if we are dealing with a lost cause. The more we invest, the greater the sunk costs are, and the greater the urge to continue becomes.

How to Recognise Whether You are a victim of Sun cost Fallacy;

When you see following behaviour in yourself while saving, spending, investing and taking insurance, it is likely that you are suffering from the sunk cost fallacy.

· Money already spent is more important and dear to you than money in the pocket. Hoping to recover the money already spent, you are ready to throw in fresh money, fully knowing and recognising the fact that the money already spent was a wrong decision.

· You prefer to sell a good investment only because it's making a profit for you while holding on to bad investments since you will lose money in doing so.

· You continue with a bad insurance policy and pay further premiums just to protect the premiums which you have already paid in the past.

How to overcome Sunk Cost Fallacy

1. Admit mistakes, cut losses earlier, and exit.

2. Check for opportunity costs–cost of missing some better investments, just by keeping the money sunk in some bad investments.

3. Above all, try to be as rational as possible, plan ahead, check pros and cons, analyse and evaluate before investing the money.

ENDOWMENT EFFECT - HOLDING ON TO WHAT YOU HAVE

Holding on to what you have is a financial mistake which very few people understand and acknowledge. People overvalue what belongs to them relative to the value they would place in the same possession or situation if it belonged to someone else. This is called the endowment effect.

For example, a person will think that his son is the most intelligent or his daughter is the most beautiful girl of all. This is a very common and widely prevalent example of the endowment effect.

Examples of Endowment Effect

1. You might have bought a flat screen television for Rs.15000. But, unfortunately, you found another superior model in the market in the next few days at the same price, and hence willing to sell this TV. Fortunately, your friend will buy it from you. What price will you quote? For sure, Rs.15000. Now assume you are in your friend's shoes and he is in your position. What price will you be willing to pay to buy the TV from your friend? For sure, less than Rs.15000.

2. Once an investor buys a stock, he will be rating that stock at a higher value and unwilling to sell at a loss. They think their stocks are highly valuable.

3. Most trial offers and money-back guarantees are at work because once you have used the product for a few days and enjoy their benefits, you would like to keep it and not return to the dealer.

4. How many products and things we stack at our lofts and wardrobes and unwilling to part away with it at a discounted price ask?

5. Would you be willing to sell your bicycle–1-year-old for 30% discounted price, even if a newer bicycle of the same model sells at the same discounted price?

6. How many of you still have your old model mobile phones at home just because during the exchange offer your existing phone was asked for a steep discounted price?

One of the most costly and regrettable consequence of endowment effect is how people deal with their retirement planning. It is relatively easy to set aside small sums of money during one's earning years so as to accumulate a large retirement corpus because of the power of compounding. But many people cannot follow this basic principle. The main reason for that can be traced back to the psychological behavior of endowment effect people overvalue what they have (today's income) and fail to properly value what they could have (financially independent retired life).

How to Recognize Whether You are a Victim of Endowment Effect

When you see the following tendencies in yourself while saving, spending, investing, or taking insurance, it is likely that you are a victim of the endowment effect:

You find it very difficult to save money

You think money today is worth more than money tomorrow; you do not think of the future but always want to live and consume what you have in the present.

You believe that your investments, whether a house or a piece of art or anything else, are worth more than your neighbors.

You do not believe in retirement planning

You are always on the lookout for "trial period" or "money back" offers.

You believe investments are too risky

You can not determine the true value of your investments and always depend on others for it.

Steps to Rectify this Mistake

Always view all situations and investments with the same eye: whether it is your own or that of somebody else.

Be wary of trail period or money back offers because it is likely that the trail period might get converted into a permanent one.

Learn to do a fair assessment and determine a proper value for your assets. The value should be the same: whether you own it or your neighbour does.

Remember that retirement planning is one of the most important facets of financial planning and the gateway towards achieving financial independence.

Try to evaluate anything as objectively as possible–keeping emotions apart

Check for opportunity cost during investing–cost of holding a bleeding stock VS an excellent opportunity to buy a good business at a bargain price.

30 DAYS FINANCIAL PLANNING CHALLENGE

Become CEO of Your Financial Life

How to become CEO of your personal financial

life

In today's fast-paced financial landscape, taking charge of your personal finances is not just a necessity but a fundamental skill that can empower you in many aspects of life. Imagine being the CEO of your own financial journey, adeptly steering your resources, investments, and expenditures toward a prosperous future. This article aims to equip you with the essential strategies and insights needed to assume this pivotal role in your life. By adopting a proactive mindset, you can gain control over your financial decisions and cultivate a comprehensive plan tailored to your unique circumstances and goals. From budgeting effectively and understanding credit to investing wisely and planning for retirement, the skills you develop will not only enhance your financial literacy, but also foster confidence in your ability to navigate challenges. As you embark on this transformative journey, remember that becoming the CEO of your personal financial life involves continuous learning, strategic thinking, and disciplined execution. Whether you are just starting out or looking to refine your existing practices, this guide will provide you with the tools necessary to take command of your financial future, ensuring that you make informed choices that align with your aspirations.

Assess your current financial situation.

Understanding your current financial situation is a critical first step toward achieving your financial goals. Begin by compiling a comprehensive overview of your income, expenses, assets, and liabilities. This includes not only your salary but also any additional sources of income, such as investments or side businesses. Evaluating your monthly expenses will help you identify discretionary spending and areas where you can cut back. By creating a detailed balance sheet of your financial standing, you will gain clarity on your net worth and overall financial health.

Once you have a clear picture of your finances, it becomes easier to set realistic and measurable goals. Whether you aim to pay off debt, build an emergency fund, or save for retirement, having a defined understanding of where you currently stand will enable you to create actionable steps toward your objectives. Regularly reviewing your financial situation will also help you track your progress and make informed decisions as your circumstances evolve.

Set clear and achievable goals.

Establishing specific and attainable goals is essential for directing your financial decisions and actions. Begin by identifying what you want to achieve in both the short and long term, whether it's eliminating credit card debt, saving for a home, or preparing for retirement. Ensure that each goal is measurable, allowing you to evaluate your progress effectively. For example, instead of stating a vague intention to save money, aim to save a certain percentage of your income each month or reach a specific dollar amount in your savings account within a defined period.

After outlining your goals, prioritize them by urgency and importance to create a roadmap for financial success. Break down larger goals into smaller, more manageable milestones to accomplish along the way. By continually assessing and adjusting your goals as circumstances change, you can maintain focus and motivation, ultimately leading to more substantial financial stability and growth.

Create a detailed financial plan.

Developing a comprehensive financial plan involves a thorough analysis of your current financial situation, including income, expenses, assets, and liabilities. Start by compiling detailed records of your cash flow to understand where your money is coming from and where it is going. This will enable you to spot patterns in your spending habits, identify areas where you can cut costs, and allocate funds toward your defined goals. Incorporate tools such as budgeting apps or spreadsheets to track your progress and make informed decisions in real-time.

Assess your investment strategy by considering your risk tolerance, time horizon, and market opportunities. Diversifying your portfolio can mitigate risk while aligning with your long-term objectives. After establishing an investment framework, regularly review and adjust your plan to respond to changes in your financial situation or shifting market conditions. This proactive approach allows you to stay on track and adapt your strategy, ensuring that you remain aligned with your goals and prepared for any unforeseen challenges.

Track your income and expenses.

Maintaining a meticulous record of your financial transactions is essential for making informed decisions about your economic future. By consistently monitoring your income and expenses, you gain insights that help you understand your financial behaviors and uncover spending patterns. This awareness not only aids in identifying areas where you might be overspending but also allows you to make strategic adjustments to align your expenditures with your financial goals. Use various tools and methods, such as budgeting software or expense tracking applications, to simplify this process and ensure that your records are accurate and up-to-date.

Setting a regular review schedule for your financial records enhances your ability to stay on track. By analyzing your financial data monthly or quarterly, you can assess your progress, celebrate achievements, and identify any deviations from your plan that require attention. This discipline fosters accountability and encourages proactive management of your finances, empowering you to make timely adjustments that reflect your growing financial landscape. As you cultivate this habit, you position yourself for greater financial stability and success.

Build an emergency savings fund.

Establishing an emergency savings fund is a critical component of your financial strategy, allowing you to navigate unexpected expenses without derailing your long-term goals. Aim to set aside three to six months' worth of expenses in a readily accessible account. This fund serves as a financial buffer, providing peace of mind when faced with challenges such as medical emergencies, job loss, or urgent home repairs. To build this safety net, consider automating your savings by scheduling regular transfers from your checking account to your emergency fund. This approach not only simplifies the process but also helps cultivate a habit of saving consistently.

Besides setting savings goals, prioritize the purpose and accessibility of your emergency fund. Keep your money in a high-yield savings account or money market account that allows for easy withdrawals while earning interest. Avoid the temptation to dip into this fund for non-emergent expenses; establishing clear guidelines on what makes up an emergency will help you maintain its integrity. By cultivating a robust emergency savings fund, you empower yourself to tackle unforeseen circumstances with confidence, ultimately steering your financial journey toward stability and resilience.

Reduce and manage your debt.

A crucial aspect of your financial health involves taking a proactive stance on debt management. Begin by organizing your debts, listing them by amount, interest rate, and due dates. This will provide clarity on your obligations and help you prioritize which debts to tackle first. Implementing a strategy, such as the avalanche or snowball method, can make the repayment process more systematic and less overwhelming. The avalanche method focuses on paying off debts with the highest interest rates first, while the snowball method emphasizes paying off smaller debts to build momentum and motivation.

Besides strategic repayment, consider negotiating with creditors to explore options such as lower interest rates or more flexible payment terms. This approach can help reduce your overall debt burden and ease financial stress. Keeping your credit utilization low and making timely payments can improve your credit score, facilitating better borrowing conditions in the future. By diligently managing your debts, you not only free up resources for saving and investing, but also lay the groundwork for a more secure financial future.

Invest wisely for future growth.

Focusing on thoughtful and strategic investments is key to securing your financial future. Diversifying your portfolio is essential; consider allocating resources across various asset classes, such as stocks, bonds, real estate, and mutual funds. This approach not only mitigates risk but also positions you to benefit from different market conditions. Regularly assessing your investment strategy and adjusting it based on performance and your growing financial goals will ensure that you remain aligned with your long-term objectives.

Educating yourself about market trends and investment vehicles will empower you to make informed decisions. To enhance your knowledge, consider attending workshops, reading financial literature, or consulting with a financial advisor. As you grow more confident in your investment choices, it becomes easier to identify opportunities that align with your risk tolerance and financial aspirations, ultimately fostering a foundation for sustained growth and financial independence.

Continuously educate yourself about finance.

Developing a sound foundation in financial literacy is vital in navigating the complexities of personal finance. By actively seeking resources such as books, online courses, and reputable financial news, you can stay updated on economic shifts and investment strategies. Embracing continuous education not only enhances your understanding of financial concepts, but also helps you develop critical thinking skills necessary for evaluating various financial products and services. This proactive approach allows you to make choices that are better tailored to your specific needs and circumstances.

Engaging with communities focused on finance can provide valuable insights and diverse perspectives. Networking with other financially savvy individuals or taking part in discussions, whether online or in person, can expose you to new ideas and strategies. By immersing yourself in a learning environment, you cultivate a mindset geared towards growth and adaptability, ensuring you remain resilient in the face of financial challenges and opportunities alike. This commitment to lifelong learning ultimately empowers you to take control of your financial destiny.

Review and adjust your strategies.

Regularly assessing and refining your financial strategies is essential for maintaining alignment with your evolving goals and circumstances. As you gain new insights and experience, it becomes crucial to revisit your plans to identify areas that require change. This process involves critically evaluating your budget, investment portfolio, and savings plans to ensure they reflect your current priorities and market conditions. Planning helps you handle unexpected problems or good chances.

Setting aside time to reflect on your financial progress helps to keep you accountable and motivated. Tracking milestones and understanding where you stand relative to your goals allows you to celebrate successes and learn from setbacks. This reflective practice not only aids in making informed decisions but also fosters resilience as you navigate through the complexities of personal finance. As you embrace a mindset of continuous improvement, you position yourself to make strategic adjustments that enhance your overall financial well-being.

Celebrate your financial milestones and achievements.

Recognizing and celebrating your financial milestones is a vital part of your journey toward achieving greater financial well-being. Acknowledging these achievements, whether big or small, reinforces your commitment to your financial goals and serves as a positive affirmation of your efforts. This practice encourages you to maintain momentum, as each milestone reached acts as a stepping stone, reminding you of your progress and the capabilities you've developed along the way. By taking the time to celebrate, you cultivate a mindset of success that can propel you toward even greater accomplishments.

These celebrations provide an opportunity to reflect on the strategies and choices that led you to these milestones. Evaluating what worked well allows you to replicate successful tactics in the future while also identifying lessons learned from setbacks. This balance of recognition and reflection not only enhances your financial literacy but also strengthens your resolve to stay engaged in your personal finance journey. By integrating celebrations into your routine, you empower yourself to embrace both achievements and challenges, fostering a holistic approach to financial growth.

In conclusion, taking charge of your personal financial life is akin to stepping into the role of CEO. By setting clear goals, developing a strategic plan, and regularly reviewing your progress, you empower yourself to make informed decisions that align with your financial aspirations. Remember to educate yourself continuously and adapt to changing circumstances, as a successful CEO would. Embrace the responsibility of managing your finances with confidence, and you will not only achieve greater financial security, but also cultivate a sense of control and fulfillment in your life. As you navigate this journey, remain committed to your vision, and you'll find that becoming the CEO of your personal finances is not just a goal—it's a transformative experience.

* * *

#1 Create a Family Vision statement, Get Clarity on Life

"Start with the end in mind"–Stephen Covey in his book "Seven Habits of Highly Effective People"

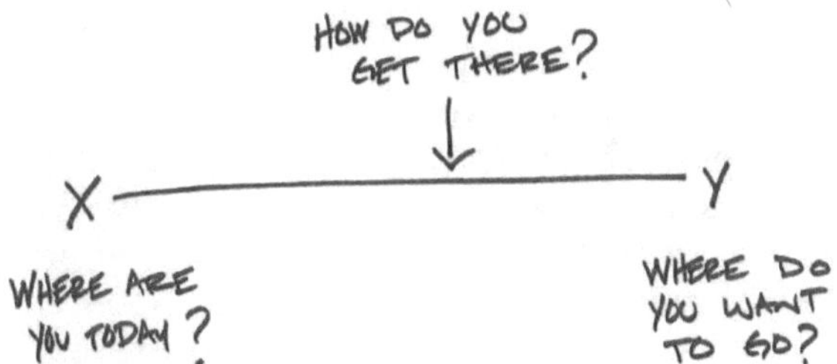

When it comes to financial planning, the "start with the end in mind" principle applies. It essentially means that you should determine what you want to achieve with your wealth, and then work backwards to create a detailed plan that will help you get there.

This principle applies to all aspects of your financial plan, from saving for retirement to investing in the stock market and planning for college fees. The reason you should start with the end in mind is that it helps you focus on the most important aspects of your financial plan. As a result, you are more likely to achieve your financial goals than if you start with a less detailed plan. When you start with the end in mind, you will have a clear idea of what you want

When we do any work, we are so focused and immersed in doing it effectively in the best way & in the least time, that we somehow lose focus on the end goal.

Have you ever thought about your life? – How you want your life to be 'x' years from now in areas life health, work, social relationships, family relationships, money, spirituality etc?

The time to do it is RIGHT NOW.

As you start on the journey of your financial wellbeing, it is fundamentally important for you and your spouse to take a break and contemplate on what is your shared vision for your family's overall wellbeing. Once you are clear on this, the work is half done.

So how to go about it? Well known Leadership Guru Robin Sharma in his wonderful book "Family Wisdom" urges families to create a family vision statement prepared jointly by all members of the family. How does it help? Firstly, a written statement is a powerful expression of intent to move forward confidently in direction of those goals. Secondly, it gives both spouses an opportunity to really sit and speak on their shared family vision, expectations & interests and helps them to come on the same page on their finances & other matters.

Lastly, this exercise gives a great deal of clarity to the family on their major life goals.

Use template bellow, take a printout if you want, convince your spouse to sit with you and fill it. You will be amazed with the kind of clarity this small exercise will bring to your financial life... because everything in life in some or the other way has an impact on your personal finances.

Family Vision Statement

(Enter your shared vision in each of the areas. Discuss it with your spouse. Write down your family's ideal scenario in each area, what you want to accomplish in each of the area)

You can download a templet from : https://links.planetwealth.in/decodedmoneyresources

<table>
<tr><td>1. Family

54

</td></tr>
<tr><td>2. Social

</td></tr>
<tr><td>3. Health

</td></tr>
<tr><td>4. Work

</td></tr>
<tr><td>5. Money

</td></tr>
<tr><td>6. Spiritual

</td></tr>
<tr><td>7. Personal

</td></tr>
</table>

#2 Make an Inventory of Your Existing Assets and Liabilities

No matter how much money you make, it is important to know how much money you have. This is basic knowledge of personal finance, and it is the first step to improving your financial situation. If you are a student, freelance worker, or other worker that does not make enough money to live off of each month, you likely live pay check to pay check. This is fine, but you should at least know how much you have in your account at any given time. Knowing how much money you have in your account can help with some of the following: - Having enough money to buy groceries for the Month. - Saving for a car, a house, or student loans. - Paying off credit card debt.

Take a moment and reflect on your financial actions to date. In most probability, one invests as a reaction to something: to get a last-minute tax deduction, giving in to a request of someone to buy a policy or buy as per the latest market trends.

There are three problems here;

Over time the investments become unwieldy, disorganized and many a times in the wrong investment avenues.

You would not want to even look back at the mess that you've created, mainly because of the time & efforts that you'll needs to put and lastly,

As Murphy's Law goes "Things, left to themselves, turn from bad to worse". Same with your investments and may cause erosion in your hard-earned wealth.

In Indian families generally men are said to assume the charge for finances. While the husband does a good (or bad, depending on case to case) job in this sphere, he doesn't realise that if suddenly something happens to him, the wife is totally clueless on where he had made the investments. Imagine for a second, while you are reading this, you get a brain haemorrhage and go in coma for 6 months. If you've never `discussed your finances with your wife, can you imagine her plight in such a case? Way out? Pick up one Sunday, skip the afternoon movie plan, and take out all your investment and insurance papers/ files/ documents. Keep your laptop beside you and use the template given below. Start keying in the details and remember that it may take you more than one sitting to close it. Once you're done, sit with your wife & explain it to her. Also show her the file that contains all the papers she can refer to.

Realise that by this simple effort of some hours, you have made life so easy for

yourself & your wife. One, you get a single view of your financial picture which makes it now very easy for you to review it/ seek suggestion from a financial advisor. Secondly,

Your wife is now aware of the family investments and you've created some kind of a financial Blackbox for her to use in case of your unfortunate death.

You may download excel template form :https://links.planetwealth.in/decodedmoneyresources

#3 Understand your Taxes, Salary Structure & Benefits

Personal finance is not only about planning and managing your money smartly, but also about understanding how your financial decisions, earnings, & benefits, affect your financial life. Whether you are already an experienced investor or you are just beginning, you have to keep in mind the fact that your earnings, benefits, & taxes have a direct impact on your financial future. Here, we'll take a look at how different factors in your salary structure, benefits package & taxes can collectively affect your financial life.

When an employee joins a new company, attached to the appointment letter is the applicable salary structure with all the components like basic salary, allowances, perquisites, reimbursements, employment benefits, deductions etc. It may be noted that each of these components is taxed in a certain way under the Income Tax Act and there are ample opportunities to structure the salary, if your company policy so provides, which can enable you to reduce the tax burden.

The needs and requirements differ from employee to employee. For e.g. for a junior level employees, the concern is to get a higher take home salary, whereby they can opt for a lower basic which will entail a lower EPF deduction. For senior level employees, since the concern is on reducing the tax impact on the higher salary they receive, they can opt for more perquisites/

reimbursements and less of fixed allowances.

Employees should also remember to adhere to timelines for submitting investment declaration (generally in April) and submission of investment proofs (generally around January). Also, care should be taken not to submit fake bills (e.g. house rent receipts, medical bills etc.) to claim reimbursements as it can backfire and land you in a problem in the future.

Another aspect of Salary Structure which most employees do not understand and fail to know its impact on financial future are Employment Benefits like Provident Fund, Superannuation, Gratuity, Group Life Insurance & Group Health Insurance. Do take time out to understand, inquire and calculate the approximate future pay-outs of each one of these components.

Simply pull out your salary structure and do an introspection of each one of the components in it. Ask your HR, friends and advisor if you do not understand the impact of any component on your financial future. You can download the illustrative ready reckoner to help you understand the tax exemptions available for salaried class.

#4 Create a Monthly & Annual Budget, Control your Expenses

Creating a budget is a great way to feel in control of your financial future and spend less than you earn. Having a plan and sticking to that plan is a great way to stay on track to financial freedom, but creating a budget doesn't have to be hard. You can easily create a monthly and annual budget in a way that works for you.

Budgeting is a way to help you get your money under control and to help you live within your means. So, what does budgeting mean? Budgeting is an organized and ongoing process that helps you spend your money wisely and live within your means. It also helps you save for the future and to reduce debts. Budgeting allows you to determine how much you can afford to spend on the things you need and want. Or a financial budget can be defined as a plan to guide and control your financial activities over a specific period, usually a year. It is used to allocate money for specific activities, such as paying for monthly bills and necessities. A personal budget can be developed for any household, regardless of income level

For a moment, think as if you are the Chief Financial Officer of a company. Now, how does the financial planning happen in a company? In the first few months of the financial year, a budget is prepared and every month, the actual cash flows are tracked against the budget to find out the variances and corrective actions are taken.

You can replicate the same in your household finances by following a 3 step process:

<u>Step 1</u>: First estimate the cash flows for every month. Given that salaries are mostly fixed, you can estimate the month on month expenses on various items and create a budget by entering the details in the "budget" columns of the template.

<u>Step 2</u>: On a daily basis, use the expense tracker sheet to enter the expenses for the day. By the end of the month, you will have the actual amount of household expenses for that month. Enter it in the cell for actual household expenses for the corresponding month.

<u>Step 3</u>: When you enter the details of actual income and expenses for every month, automatically, the excel sheet will calculate the surplus/ deficit & the variation from the budget. If the variation is adverse (that means actual savings are LESS than the budgeted savings), the amount will be shown in red font. It is here that you need to go back and check the nature of expenses for the month – were there high discretionary expenses, one off expenses etc.? Take corrective action as possible.

Framing a budget and tracking expenses on a regular basis is a powerful exercise to build awareness about your spending patterns, and take control over your spending patterns.

If you need an excel sheet to do your yearly budget, please visit https://links.planetwealth.in/decodedmoneyresources to download excel template.

#5 AUTOMATE YOUR PAYMENTS & INVESTMENTS

I magine this. You wake up in the morning and your financial worries are handled. You don't have to worry about how you'll make your monthly bills, how you'll pay for groceries, or how you'll save for retirement. You don't have to worry about how to invest your savings, how to make your money grow, or how to find better investment opportunities. All these details are handled for you. You don't even think about them. All you have to worry about is getting up, going to work, and enjoying life.

While you're moving towards taking actions for your financial wellbeing, Introducing simplicity and process orientation will help a great deal. So, instead of you being always on the move for paying this utility bill or cutting a cheque for that mutual fund investment, don't you think there is a merit in automating these simple activities?

This will help you in the following three ways:

Firstly, it will simplify your financial life by freeing up your precious time which can then be used for more productive pursuits.

Secondly, you actually can reduce instances of late payment charges, insurance policy lapses etc. and the unavoidable stress that comes with it.

Thirdly and the most important, it inculcates a savings discipline in you & lets you know how much you're left with to spend after paying all mandatory expenses and making the necessary investments for your future.

How to go about it?

You can select a particular date of the month say 5thor 10th(ideally within a week of salary credit in your account) & set up an Electronic Clearing Service (ECS) mandate on the following payments:

- Your utility payments like telephone, mobile, internet, gas, electricity, etc.
- Your credit card bill payments
- Your mutual fund investments (SIPs)
- Your insurance premium payments (if payment mode is monthly)
- Your loan EMIs
- For utilities, you will have to get the ECS form verified from your bank and submit to the utility company.

This is all a onetime setup, a tedious process but once set, you will be at peace. So take the initiative to automate most of you investments and payments.

#6 Build and Park your Emergency Fund

For many people, emergencies are an inevitable part of life. And although we can't always predict what will happen, we can prepare for it. Building an emergency fund is one of the best ways to get yourself financially ready for anything that could come up, because it gives you a buffer between you and financial catastrophe. If you find yourself in a situation where you need a loan, one of the best places to get it is from your emergency fund. You can use your cash to create a solid financial foundation that will help you achieve financial freedom moving forward.

When you create an investment plan for your financial goals, it's like you are creating a building. But have you thought about what can happen to a building if it does not have a foundation?

Your emergency fund is such a foundation. Emergency fund is a specific amount depending on your need and requirement that you need to set aside in liquid instruments, so that it can be redeemed quickly in case of an emergency.

It ensures that when you make investments systematically for your financial goals, any short term emergencies like a job loss, or a medical emergencies in family, natural calamities etc does not let the plan fall off the track. In such unfortunate events, your emergency fund ensures that you are able to pay for your regular expenses, your utlity bills, EMI's on time and you need not stop your SIPs for your financial goals.

Also, a proper emergency fund ensures that you do not fall in the trap of high interest credit card debt or personal loans.

Coming to how much emergency fund you should have, it can be anywhere between 6- 12 months of your fixed monthly obligations, which includes your household expenses, dependent expenses, loan EMIs and monthly SIPs.

The amount should be reviewed periodically and topped up if there is a shortfall.

You can place your emergency fund in one of the following avenues:

1. **Liquid mutual fund**
2. **Short term Bank FDs**

#7 Ensure you have Required Life Insurance Cover

Financial freedom is the ability to use your time how you want, without having to work for someone else. Wealthy people don't need to work in order to earn an income. They can enjoy their time for things that they love to do. However, the freedom to choose when to work and when to play comes with a price. Wealthy people have to work for it. They have to earn it. And they have to protect it. One of the best ways to protect your wealth is with life insurance.

The desire for financial freedom is what drives many to work as hard as they can to build their wealth. But this is not without its risks—if a person dies prematurely, their family may lose a substantial amount of money that could have been used to pay for things like education or health care. That's why it's important to consider your financial future and plan for it by purchasing adequate life insurance to protect you and your family.

Life insurance has just one purpose: In case something happens to you, your family should get a lump sum amount so that there is zero financial impact in your absence.

So, three points deserve attention when you're looking for buying life insurance:

a) Buy the right product type

b) Ensure that your life insurance cover is of sufficient amount

c) Select the right life insurance company based on track record.

So, when you talk about the right product type, understand that pure term insurance is the only right product to buy. Traditional/ ULIPs are not suitable for getting enough / large insurance cover and it is advisable not to mix insurance with investments.

Consumers often confuse "premium" for "sum assured", It is the "sum assured" that your family will get in case of your death.

Though there is a growing awareness of term insurance, its common to see consumers arbitrarily choosing the amount of life insurance cover which may fall short when its needed or being under a wrong presumption that they are adequately covered, thus defeating the very purpose of getting life insurance.

A life insurance cover should be enough to pay off your outstanding liabilities, help your family meet financial goals when due, and be enough to create a regular income stream for the family to meet the household expenses. You can take help of the below calculator to find out how much life insurance you should purchase. Also, it's recommended to review your life insurance requirements once a year.

When you're checking as to which company to buy, don't procrastinate by waiting for the best product or best company. Go with an insurance company you're comfortable with keeping in mind their reputation and general word on claims settlement & service standards and pricing.

Remember that insurance is a contract of utmost good faith so honestly disclose all material facts about your health and existing policies at the time of application to avoid issues at the time of claim. Do not forget to nominate your spouse/relative.

Please download life insurance calculator from here : https://links.planetwealth.in/decodedmoneyresources

#8 Purchase your Own Mediclaim / Health Insurance

The next step in financial freedom is to purchase your own health insurance and stop paying someone else to take care of you. You might want to consider this if you are self-employed, working for a small company, or you just want to be able to choose your own doctors and treatment plans. On the other hand, purchasing your own insurance qualifies you for tax breaks and you will always have a say in what kind of coverage you want.

Let us today discuss about Mediclaim insurance. Mediclaim insurance is again a risk cover whereby the insurance company reimburses the medical expenses in case of a hospitalisation of the insured. This is a must have cover, so that you can cover yourself & family from the financial costs of hospitalisation & especially in view of ever-increasing cost of medical treatment nowadays, especially in metro cities.

One common query that employees have is that they are anyway covered under their employer's group Mediclaim cover. Does it then make sense to purchase own cover?

Answer is **YES**, and because of the following reasons:

 # 1: Possibility of arbitrary changes in policy terms by employer where you don't have any say

 # 2: The cover amount from the company may not be enough for you

 # 3: your Hospitalisation in the "breakperiod" between jobs is not covered

 # 4: Difficulty in getting health insurance later in life after you quit full time employment (precisely the time when you need it the most)

So, it makes a lot of sense to buy your own medical insurance cover. While selecting the policy, first look at the features and comprehensiveness of the policy & then compare premiums. The new IRDA health insurance regulations have made health policies much more consumer friendly with features like lifelong renewal, no loading on claims & mandatory free look period.

Also, if you already have a mediclaim insurance, do check if it is of sufficient amount. For e.g. in metro cities, a cover less than Rs. 10 lac is a cause for concern. It is here that you can look at super topup plans which come at a very low cost & trigger only if the claim exceeds the amount of the existing insurance cover.

#9 Buy a Personal Accident Policy. It's Cheap!

Buying a personal accident policy is a great way to create financial freedom. A personal accident policy will help you to protect your family's assets in case you or a family member are incapacitated by an accident. Your family won't have to worry about losing their house or going into debt if something happens to you -- they'll still be able to maintain their standard of living.

Usually, there is adequate promotion and awareness by media about life insurance and health insurance, but where a lot of people are still unaware is "personal accident insurance". Now imagine for a second, you're walking down the road one day & suddenly, a carelessly driving biker rams into you.

When you open your eyes, you're in hospital bed, bruised & to your shock; you discover that your one hand & one leg had to be amputated. As you come to terms with how life has suddenly changed for you, you realise that you may not be gainfully employed for the rest of your life as others do. Another shocking realisation: your life insurance will not pay as you are still alive, & your mediclaim will pay only till you're in the hospital. But what about the moment that you're out of the hospital & into the world?

How will you & your family survive?

Here is where personal accident policies come into picture. A personal accident policy covers permanent/ partial disabilities and pays a lump sum amount according to the type of disability that one incurs. And then there are extensive products that even cover broken bones, transportation of mortal remains, purchase of blood etc. Ideally, your personal accident cover should not be any less than the life insurance requirement however, please note that insurance companies put a cap on sum assured as a specified number of times (usually 10) of your gross annual income.

Personal Accident policies are very cheap. The premium depends on your class of occupation (how risky it is). For e.g. a personal accident cover of Rs. 50 lacs along with a temporary total disability cover of Rs. 5 lacs will cost you only around Rs. 5,700 per annum.

#10 List down Your Family's Financial Goals

Money is a topic that many people have a hard time talking about. (It's awkward when you don't have any, right?) The advice you get from family and friends is often conflicting, and many of us never learn how to manage our finances. But what if you started your financial journey by coming up with a list of your financial goals? This isn't a step most financial planners will tell you to do, but it's a great way to get a clear picture of your financial future—and to make sure you're heading down a path that gets you where you want to be.

Having a plan is critical to achieving your financial goals, but knowing what your goals are is even more important. If you don't know where you're going, how can you possibly know when you arrive? That is why it is so important to create a financial plan that not only incorporates your financial goals, but focuses on the most important aspects of your life that you want to achieve them with. By creating your financial goals and creating a plan that incorporates those goals, you'll be able to better prioritize your money and your life.

So, once you have fixed your emergency fund and insurance requirements, we come to planning for your financial goals. So till date, you've invested as a "reaction" to something – maybe to get tax deduction, maybe someone requested you to purchase so that he/she can meet the sales targets, whatever. Yes, there has always been an underlying intention to plan and save some amount regularly towards your financial goals, but most likely those goals are somewhere in thin air & not much thought has gone to crystalline them.

As you might have felt while drawing up the family vision statement, you get a good sense of clarity on your financial goals. Now, it's the time to actually write them down the precise financial goal, when you'll need the funds & an estimated amount.

So, if you have a vague idea of purchasing a car some years down the line, it has no value. BUT, if you say you wish to purchase a car (say a sedan) having an onroad price today at 6 lacs in 2018, that's what is a financial goal.

How does listing down financial goals help? In the following ways:

a. Gives a lot of clarity on money requirements that are due in near future as well as long term so that the right planning can be done.

b. Different goals require different kinds of planning. Planning for a short-term goal is very different from planning from a long term one. A financial goals listing helps the investor takes the right decisions on where & how much to invest so that the goals are met.

Click https://links.planetwealth.in/ decodedmoneyresources for financial goals articulation template.

#11 Assign Each One of Your Investments with a Life Goal

Investing is something that most of us need to do in order to achieve financial freedom. When investing, it is important to make sure you are always evaluating your portfolio and deciding on a course of action. You may be able to make some money, but if you are not going to be able to use it for the future, then it's not doing you a lot of good. Sometimes, you have to change your investment strategy in order to give it the best chances of success. You have to decide whether it's time for you to be in a more aggressive or conservative stance. If you're not sure, then you may need to change things up. If you're going to change

When it comes to creating financial freedom, there is no one-size-fits-all approach. Many people look to earn as much as they can so that they can save the most they can. Others, however, may be happy with a mid-level salary, as long as they are able to take care of their families. If you are in the latter group, it can still be harder than you expect to allocate your investments in a way that will allow you to retire comfortably. One option is to assign each one of your investments with a life goal to create financial freedom.

So, now that you've really zeroed in on your financial goals, refer your assets inventory that you must have made at the start of the course. Now is the time to tag the investments to your life goals.

How this will help? See, the main reason one is not able to continue with the investment plan is due to the lack of direction & wrong choice of financial products. When you tag your assets to a goal, it will instil a great sense of responsibility towards your financial well being & will resist the temptation to liquidate the funds which are earmarked to a financial goal.

For e.g. you've been consistently investing a certain amount per month through SIP.

Some years down the line, if you've consciously tagged this investment to your child's education goal, you'll feel less inclined to withdraw it for buying a sedan or going on a vacation or lending that money to relatives & friends when they knock the door.

While you do this activity, keep a tab on the expected maturity of the investment underlying intention is to find the best match between due year of the goal vis a vis maturity year of the asset that you are looking to tag to the goal.

Below table broadly lays down the right way to tag the financial goals to the assets:

1. Short Term Goals (Less than 3 years) Fixed Deposit, Liquid fund, Cash & Bank

Balances

2. Medium term goals (3 to 6 Years) FD/ RD, Debt & MIP Mutual funds

3. Long term goals (6 Years +) Direct Equity, Equity Mutual funds, PPF, EPF, Insurance cum Investment Plans, NPS

#12 Avoid These 'N' Common Investment Mistakes

In the investing journey, there are some common mistakes that if avoided, can make a material difference in the amount of corpus one accumulates and more importantly, saves one from the guilt & pain that come with having realised the mistakes.

Some of the common mistakes done by investors are listed as follows:

Mixing insurance with investments: Every day, we are bombarded with advertisements for new investment products. These new products claim to be the next big thing, and that by combining your investment and insurance needs, they will allow you to reach your financial goals faster. While this sounds like a great idea, the reality is that combining these financial products can have a negative impact on your financial well-being. The reason is simple. Your investment and insurance goals are very different, and mixing these two types of financial products together can lead to unnecessary costs and increased risk of losing money. When you work with a qualified financial planner, you can create an investment portfolio that matches your individual goals and risk tolerance, and a separate life insurance plan that meets your needs.

<u>Investing without a proper asset allocation</u>: As you may or may not know, financial planning is a complex subject. Because managing your money requires a lot of upfront work, it can feel like you are in over your head before you even start. That's why it's important to only invest in something you understand. This is a mistake a lot of people make when it comes to financial planning. If you don't have a solid grasp on your asset allocation, you could easily lose money.

<u>Overleveraging your income</u>(e.g. taking huge loans to fund real estate purchases): Overleveraging can be defined as acquiring a loan that is greater than what you need. Although it may seem like a great idea at the time, this strategy is usually a recipe for financial disaster. While it may seem like a good idea to purchase a home or a car with extra money, the truth is that it is a big financial mistake. This strategy is called overleveraging, and it is a bad idea because it puts you at financial risk. Another example of overleveraging is using credit cards to pay for items that you don't own yet. If you have to wait until you receive your paycheck to pay off your credit card

<u>Investing for long term goals without creating a contingency fund & planning for short term goals</u> : Most people have short term goals and long term goals. Short term goals can typically be achieved in a 2-3 year time frame, while long term goals can range anywhere from 5-10 years or more. A lot of times people will plan to work towards both of these goals at the same time, while not planning to create a contingency fund. A contingency fund is exactly what it sounds like, a fund that is prepared in case of emergency. If you have a long term goal that you want to reach for, but you have not planned for short term goals or a contingency fund, then you could risk losing everything if something happens, and not reach your final goal.

Running after the next rabbit that crosses your path(investing in the latest IPO or mutual fund NFO or latest real estate scheme) : Running after the next new investment, the next hot stock tip from a friend or the next best way to invest your money is a habit that will take a firm hold on your finances. If you've ever tried chasing this rabbit, you know that it never leads to a place you want to go - to a financially secure future. Let us show you how to put an end to this foolish behavior, and to start living the life you really want.

Overdiversification in case of mutual fund schemes(investing in too many MF schemes): In India, it is common for people to have multiple mutual fund (MF) schemes in their portfolio. While diversification is a good thing, investing in too many MF schemes is not. Typically, one should invest in not more than five to six MF schemes

Investing in direct equity/ derivatives without adequate knowledge/ professional advice and also inclination Investing out of line with one's risk taking ability: One of the biggest mistakes that people make when investing is they don't know how to assess their risk level. If you understand your risk level, you will be able to make better decisions about your investments and where to invest your money. A big part of assessing your risk level is knowing what your tolerance for risk is. If you answer honestly about your tolerance for risk, you will likely have a better return on your investment.

Not tracking the portfolio performance on a periodic basis & sticking with poor performing schemes: Many people are of the mind that keeping a close eye on their portfolio is a waste of time. As long as they are investing in proven, well-performing assets, they say, they can leave their investments alone. This might be the worst mistake they can make.

Instead of doing nothing, you need to actively manage your portfolio to ensure it is properly diversified, properly allocated, and properly positioned to take advantage of market opportunities (and guard against threats).

Investing in instruments which give a negative real return (i.e. return after adjusting for inflation) like Fixed Deposits: Investing without evaluating real returns will hurt your financial well-being. The reason is that not all investments are created equal. Some will give you a good return and some will give you a bad return. To evaluate a return you should look at both the nominal return and the real return. The nominal return is the percent change in the value of an investment. The real return is the percent change in the value of an investment after taking into account the effects of inflation and tax.

Investing without an eye on tax efficiency of investment (for e.g. a person in a 30% tax bracket is better off investing in debt mutual funds than fixed deposit, in view of taxability) : In general, investing is a great way to grow your money. However, there are certain ways you need to approach investing if you want to make the most of it. One such way is to be tax efficient. You see, by being tax efficient you will make sure that you are not penalized for taking the money out or being penalized for merely holding onto it. The question you need to ask yourself is how do you invest in a way that is tax efficient?

Investing when markets are high & redeeming when markets are low(not investing systematically) : Investing systematically is a methodical way of investing in the stock market or real estate market. It is based on the assumption that most people are not good at timing the market or knowing when to get out. By investing systematically, you can take advantage of a market downturn without worrying about your money when the market is low.

<u>Locking all money in long term products</u>(e.g. PPF, life insurance policies etc.) – as a result when money is required in short term, one is forced to take a personal loan :

As a finance writer, I get to see a lot of bad financial decisions being made—especially by people just starting out or looking to make a big change in their situation. One of the most common mistakes I see is that people underestimate the importance of liquidity. If you have a cash crunch, you need to have access to cash—and if you don't have cash on hand, you could find yourself in a really bad situation.

You may well check if you are presently making these mistakes & if yes, take corrective action in time else simply prevent making these mistakes.

#13 RUN A PEST CONTROL ON YOUR PERSONAL FINANCE

L ike we do a pest control regularly at our home to ensure they are germ free, it makes good sense to also do a periodic pest control on personal finances as well.

A pest control kind of exercise will ensure that unnecessary & nonperforming

investments are weeded out, wherever your money is lying is obtained, & your financial portfolio is simplified for better monitoring & tracking.

1. Close unnecessary bank accounts especially the salary account once you've changed jobs

2. Transfer your EPF balance from previous employers

3. Close unnecessary MF folios

4. Correct your email ID and other details in your investments

5. Update your change of address and/ or residential status in your investments/insurance policies

6. Apply for unclaimed amounts in mutual funds/ insurance companies

7. Update the emergency file with latest information

8. Close unnecessary credit cards and debit cards

9. Close any unnecessary ECS mandates given on your bank account

10. Change the passwords for bank accounts etc. for security reasons if you have'nt changed for long time

11. Review MF performance and take necessary action

12. Review and update nominations in all your financial and physical assets

#14 Get Disciplined. Start a SIP in Mutual Fund

Mutual fund investments are a great way to reduce the risk by diversification as well as benefit from professional fund management, for a small fee.

The most recommended way to invest in mutual funds, especially for those who have a regular fixed income, is through a systematic investment plan, popularly known as SIP.

SIP is a common way that wealth is created by the Indian middle class, as they tend to invest in mutual funds to grow their wealth.

Systematic investment plans or SIPs are an intelligent way to invest in mutual fund schemes that can help investors ride out market volatility. A SIP allows you to invest in a mutual fund scheme on a fixed date every month, every week, or every day. This is usually done through money-management softwares. It's a good way to invest a fixed amount of money every month, and to do it regularly. (This will make the investment very disciplined and more importantly, systematic. This is a good thing.)

Investing through SIP in mutual funds allows you to invest a certain predetermined amount at a regular interval (weekly, monthly, quarterly, etc.). This regular investing approach helps you build the necessary discipline towards wealth creation and setting aside a fixed amount every month towards your long term financial goals.

How can you set up an SIP? Just approach your financial advisor& fill the SIP application form along with a cancelled cheque of your bank account from which you need the amount to be debited on a regular basis. You'll also need to mention the date & frequency of debit. Ideally, you should select a date in the first week of the month & frequency as monthly. Once it is activated, money is autodebited from your bank account and invested into a specific mutual fund scheme and you are allocated certain number of units based on the ongoing market rate (called NAV or net asset value) for the day.

SIP is greatly helpful in terms of averaging the cost of your investment in volatile markets and bringing in the necessary discipline and process orientation in your saving and investing. SIP is the most popular and effective way for retail investors to participate and benefit from the equity markets.

Investing in mutual funds can be a great way to grow your wealth over time. However, with so many different options available, it can be difficult for individuals to decide which fund is the best for them. Knowing the various types of mutual funds and understanding the various criteria for choosing a fund can help you make informed decisions and select a fund that meets your needs and your financial goals. We will discuss how to identify the best mutual fund for investing, including what to consider when evaluating a fund, the different types of mutual funds and how to research a fund before investing. By the end, you will have the knowledge and the confidence to make an informed decision when it comes to choosing the right mutual fund for your investments.

1. Analyze your financial goals

Before selecting the best mutual fund to invest in, it's important to analyze your financial goals. Ask yourself: What are my financial goals? How much do I need to save for retirement? How much can I afford to save each month? What types of returns do I expect from my investments? Answering these questions will help you determine the type of mutual fund that best fits your needs. Once you've identified your financial goals, you can begin researching and selecting the mutual funds that are most likely to help you reach them.

2. Research the different types of mutual funds

Before investing in any mutual fund, it is important to research the different types of mutual funds available. Mutual funds come in many shapes and sizes, including stock funds, bond funds, money market funds, and index funds. Each type has its own advantages and disadvantages, so it is important to understand the differences and decide which type of fund is best for your individual investing needs. Once you understand the different types of mutual funds, you can begin researching individual funds to find the one that best fits your goals.

3. Compare fees and performance

After you have narrowed your choice of mutual funds down to a few that match your risk-return profile, it's time to compare their fees and performance. Each mutual fund will have a different set of fees, such as an annual management fee and a fee for buying or selling shares. Some funds even charge a fee if you don't meet certain investment criteria. It's important to look closely at the fees structure of each fund you're considering so you can compare and decide which one is the best for you. Additionally, you should look at the performance of each mutual fund to ensure that it is meeting your expectations. You can find the performance of any mutual fund by checking out the fund's website or looking at independent investment research sites.

4. Develop a diversified portfolio

One of the most important elements of choosing the best mutual fund is developing a diversified portfolio. This means you want to invest in different asset classes, such as stocks, bonds, real estate, and cash. It's also wise to diversify within each asset class, so that you're not overexposed to any particular sector or company. This will provide greater stability to your portfolio and help reduce your overall risk. When choosing the best mutual fund, you want to make sure that it offers a range of investments to ensure you're diversified.

5. Consult with a financial advisor

If you are new to investing, you may find it beneficial to consult with a financial Planner. A financial planner can help you assess your financial goals, your income, and your risk tolerance. They can also provide advice on which mutual funds are appropriate for your individual needs and give you guidance on how to monitor and adjust your investments over time. A financial advisor can also help you understand the various fees that accompany mutual funds so that you can make an informed decision when selecting the best mutual fund for your needs.

Ultimately, selecting the best mutual fund for your investment goals and needs involves doing your research, understanding the investment objectives of the different funds available, and considering the associated fees and tax implications. By taking the time to understand the different types of mutual funds, the risks associated with each, and the fees charged, you can ensure that you make an informed decision about which mutual fund best suits your investment needs.

#15 Get Comfortable with Equity & Stock Markets

A major reason why most of the wealth is concentrated in fixed deposits, real estate and gold is because investors do not feel comfortable and understand how equity as an asset class works.

If you devote some dedicated time towards tracking equity market returns and volatility over various periods, you'll realise that equity over long term is very much less risky and delivers superior inflation adjusted returns vis a vis gold, deposits and real estate.

Also, unlike other assets, returns from equity commands a lesser holding period of 1 year & long term capital gains from equity are relatively low tax that go a long way towards securing your financial goals.

There are a few strategies to get comfortable with equity markets:

1. **Do not invest directly in stock markets and instead opt for the mutual fund route.**
2. **You can start off with a balanced fund that has a sizeable allocation to fixed income instruments and are less volatile than the pure equity fund.**
3. **Do not invest lumpsum – invest systematically by way of small amounts every**
4. **month with the Systematic Investment Plans (SIPs)**

5. **Do not invest in a lot of MF schemes. Restrict yourself to mutual fund schemes which have a proven track record of performance and strong fund house pedigree.**

It's easy to get started with equity investments but difficult to stay invested due to market volatility. But once you understand and appreciate that equity markets always move up in the long term, you will have the wherewithal to remain invested and participate in superior returns that equity markets deliver in long term.

Get hold of a good financial advisor who will stand by you and keep guiding you during the market ups and downs.

#16 Make sure your Investments beat the Inflation

When consumers save and invest for their long term financial goals, it is not enough to save a fixed amount every month & invest. It is critical to deploy the savings in instruments which yield higher than the prevailing inflation.

Let us take an example. Suppose, you invest Rs. 100 today which gives you say 10% annual return. Now, this 10% is nominal return. When you factor in inflation at say 7%, the "real return" that you've got is like this: $\{(1+10\%)/(1+7\%)\}1 = 2.80\%$

So, when you make investments, you've to be cautious that as your investments grow,the silent monster of inflation also catches up. Hence, your overall portfolio should earn you atleast an amount over & above the inflation, or say a positive real return.

How to achieve that? By including some amount of equity in your portfolio as per your comfort level. While fixed income investments like FD and debt funds give stability, equity MF in the portfolio will bring the much needed growth push so that your portfolio beats inflation in the long term.

Click   Here   https://links.planetwealth.in/decodedmoneyresources to download excel template to calculate your portfolio's real retrun.

#17 Leverage on Power of Compounding in Investments

In one of the earlier chapters,we discussed about Systematic Investment Plan (SIP) in mutual funds & how if you start SIP early on in your career & continue investing for longer time frames like 5, 10, 15, 20 years, your investments benefit from the tremendous power of compounding.

Example

If you started investing Rs. 10,000 a month on your 40th birthday, assuming a rate of return of 8%, in 15 years time you would have accumulated Rs. 59.29 lakhs. However, if you had started earlier say at 25 and continued investing half the SIP amount i.e. Rs. 5,000 per month till 60 years, you'll be able to build a corpus of Rs. 1.15 CR which is almost double than the Rs. 59.29 lacs.

This is the power of compounding! Albert Einstein called it the 8th wonder of the world for good reasons.

Start Age	End Age	Monthly SIP	Total Invested Amt	Total Corpus
40	60	10,000	24,00,000	59,29,000
25	60	5,000	21,00,000	1,15,46,000

So, please be mindful of the fact that the earlier you start with your investments (and don't worry, you can start off with small amounts & increase it later as your income increases), your portfolio will start gaining from the power of compounding and the longer your horizon of investment, the more magnified will be the benefits and the corpus at the end of the period.

#18 Try to Take the Loan Burden off Your Head

Now that you've streamlined the investments part, we'll come to loans. Make a list of all the loans you've taken from people – be it banks, NBFCs, credit card, friends, relatives etc.

Loan may be of following types:

1) <u>Secured loans</u> (like loan for purchase of house property, car loan, gold loan etc.)

2) **Unsecured Loans** (personal loan, credit card outstanding, loans from relatives)

Now, it is important to realise that when you take a loan, you are leveraging your future income for present consumption which is a very risky thing to do. At one end, companies launch new products and on the other hand, there are ready loans available at very high rates of interest.

Whereas one should strive to close any open loan/ liability at the earliest as and when funds are available, the issue comes when there are multiple loans and resultant confusion as to which loan to close first. Here, you should first try to close unsecured loans which have a high rate of interest and no tax benefits.

So, for example, a personal loan comes at > 15% interest with zero tax benefit whereas a home loan comes with ~ 11% interest AND tax benefits on repayment of principal and interest. It is here that one should first apply the money to personal loan and then look at home loan.

Once you close off the loan, it is also very important to obtain the closure letter and check CIBIL report after a few months whether the loan is shown as closed or not.

Also, you can check the below calculator to prepare a loan amortisation schedule and find out how much amount is outstanding at a given point in time so as to plan prepayment/ foreclosure.

#19 Avoid taking Loans or creating Liabilities

The steady rise in consumerism in a past 10 to 15 years means you can get a loan very easily for almost anything and everything. When we talk about buying things on loan, it's a very carefully designed sales strategy where the consumer does not initially feel the pinch in terms of financial outgo, however the total outgo over a time including the interest amount sometimes is more than twice or thrice the cost of the product.

Also, due to the aggressive campaigns, people tend to overleverage their income by buying things on loan. And over time, as the 2008 recession showed us, when things turn worse, people start faltering on their loan payments, which start impacting their credit score & worse, results in repossession of house/car etc. by the financing company which becomes a big source of emotional loss & can even lead one to depression.

Moreover, during the continuity of loan, there is a constant stress and anxiety over whether one will be able to service the loan obligations or not.

Hence, the best way out is to plan things in advance and resist the temptation to buy things on loan/ by way of a credit card etc. Just because loan is available is not a good reason to go for it. Here let us point out what are good loans (recommended) and bad loans (avoidable)

Good Loans (Recommended)
1. Home Loan
2. Business Loan
3. Education Loan

Bad Loans (Avoidable)
1. Credit Card
2. Car Loans
3. Personal Loan
4. EMI Option of Smartphones, Whitegoods, International Vacations etc
5. Borrowing from friends and relatives

#20 Don't Get Trapped by Credit Card Companies

Credit cards or plastic money is the way to go today. From online purchases to even shopping at malls, consumers do not mind paying via credit card. The primary reason is that paying by credit card pinches less as there is no immediate monetary outgo.

Secondly, there is a free credit period and reward points. But the sad part of the whole story is that where the credit card usage is now rampant, people are not aware of how to use them properly which results in large overdue outstanding, negative impact on credit score, harassment by credit card companies etc.

Some simple steps one can take so as not to get trapped by credit card companies is as follows:

To the extent possible, DO NOT use credit cards. Just keep 1 or 2 credit cards at the max. and close all unnecessary cards.

On the online shopping websites, pay by netbanking.

While purchasing offline, use debit card. It will help you gain control over the cash flow position & control your spending habits.

When your credit card payment is due, pay the "total balance" and not the

"minimum balance" – reason, when you make the minimum balance payment, a hefty interest is levied on the balance amount.

Schedule an ECS/ standing instruction for credit card payment, ideally in the first week of the month itself. This will ensure that there are no instances of late payments which attract interest/ late fees & negatively impact your credit score.

Every month, when you receive the credit card statement, do make it a point to check the credit card statement & raise any errors with the credit card company

Check your CIBIL score on a yearly basis as to any credit cards which are closed/ not in your name are reflected as open.

#21 CHECK YOUR CREDIT SCORE AND MAINTAIN A HEALTHY SCORE

Whenever you do any credit activity, like purchasing on your credit card, settling the card bill, take or service your home/ personal/ other loan, or even a simple activity like inquiring for the best loan with the lowest rates, you must know that the activity is getting monitored and recorded in a repository by a credit bureau called CIBIL.

CIBIL collects and maintains records of an individual's payments pertaining to loans and credit cards. These records are submitted to CIBIL by banks and other lenders, on a monthly basis. This information is then used to create Credit Information Reports (CIR) and credit scores which are provided to lenders in order to help evaluate and approve loan applications.

The report rates each individual on a score of 300 to 900. As a general rule, anything above 750 is considered acceptable but anything below 700 is considered negative.

When you visit a bank to apply for a loan/ credit card, bank checks your CIBIL report.

A report showing issues/ low score can even lead to a rejection of loan.

According to CIBIL, following are the ways to maintain a healthy score:

1. **Always pay your dues on time**
2. **Keep your balances low**
3. **Monitor your cosigned,**
4. **guaranteed and joint accounts monthly**
5. **Review you credit history frequently throughout the year**
6. **Purchase your CIR (Credit Information Report) from time to time to avoid unpleasant surprises in the form of a rejected loan application**

You can apply for your credit report at CIBIL website. It will cost you Rs. 500/.

After you receive the report, thoroughly check if for any issues which you'll need to raise with CIBIL and get rectified. It is recommended to review the report on a yearly basis to avoid any unpleasant surprises on this front.

#22 Utilize Tax Benefits available & File taxes on time

Often, we are either complacent or ignorant that we do not care for and take benefit of the various tax benefits that are available to us. The tax benefits can be broken down in the following manner:

Structure your salary for maximum tax advantage

Do not miss the company timeline as regards filing investment declaration (around April-May) and submitting investment proofs & bills for claiming reimbursements (around Dec-Jan every year)

A common mistake people make is non disclosure of income apart from salary (for e.g. house property income, bank interest, any capital gains on share transactions & mutual funds etc.). It can cause a problem later on & you might have to pay penalty for concealment of income.

In case of capital gains, develop an understanding of the exemptions you can claim and time limits for investing in new asset, to avoid paying unnecessary capital gains tax

File your returns in time – usually, it is July 31 for individual assesses every year. You can file yourself on the dedicated efiling website, or check online portals like Cleartax or Taxspanner or hire a qualified CA/ CFP/ CWM professional to do it for you.

Understand your obligation of paying advance tax and when it is to be paid – check this calculator on Income

Tax website

In case any self assessment tax is due, you can pay through this link

Before filing tax returns, you must check the credit for tax deducted at source in Form 26AS (link to view/ download Form 26AS is available when you login on Income Tax efiling website)

#23 Ensure you have Nominated Your Loved Ones

When we make any investment, we are in such a hurry to close so many things that one very important thing forgotten is making a nomination. Nomination is a great facility to ensure that the nominated person is able to receive the money from an insurance / investment in case of your death. The nominee does not become the absolute owner orthe money but holds it under trust for your legal heirs. A nomination can be changed any number of times.

Also, it is often observed that a person may nominate parents before marriage and after getting married, he might wish to change the nomination to wife. Also, there might be a case that the nominee has expired and hence a fresh nomination in the name of a new person should be made.

Nomination can be done in insurance policies, bank accounts, PPF, EPF, NPS, Fixed/Recurring Deposits, Mutual funds, Bonds, Demat account,Bank Lockers etc.

So, it's highly advised to review the nominations existing in all current investments,bank accounts& insurance policies to see if they are existing and proper. If no, one should register/ change the same with the concerned company. Also, care should be taken to align the nominations in line with the "will" so that there is a minimum scope for conflict at a later stage.

#24 Prepare a Will, Just in Case...

Generally, when we speak of will, the perception is something for a very old person or a very wealthy person who wants to distribute the wealth within a joint family. This is incorrect.

So, if today you were to die and you don't have a will (it is known as died intestate), your wealth/ property shall be divided as per the Hindu Succession Act, 1956/ Indian Succession Act, 1925 which prescribes the method of division between the various relatives.

In such a case, in absence of a nomination or a joint ownership, your spouse or family may face considerable difficulty getting moneys from banks and financial institutions who will insist on a probated copy of will or a succession certificate from the court to release the money. Also, to get a succession certificate is a complex legal procedure and takes a good six months to one year of time as well as spending advocate's fee and court charges.

To avoid this hardship, it is advisable to create a simple will. The will should list down details of your physical and financial assets and whom you want to bequeath them to.

The will should be dated, signed, preferably typed, and should contain signatures of 2 witnesses in your presence. The original copy of the will can be stored in a safe place/ locker & a copy of it can be given to one of the witnesses/ close friend.

For making a will, you can check out online portals like Willjini or can consult an Advocate/ CA/ CWM professional who can do it for you. You should also make it a point to review the will on a yearly basis to keep it up to date.

#25 Prepare your Money Emergency Kit

So you have prepared yourself well by taking the right insurance covers, nominating your loved ones and even have put a will in place. Now, despite having done all this, if your spouse is not aware of your investments or insurance policies or what steps to take in case there is an emergency, most of the good effort will go down the drain.

Hence, it's a good idea is to prepare a money emergency kit. This money emergency kit will contain details of the persons to contact in case of emergency, your financial planner, CA, lawyer, family physician etc. Also, it will tell precisely where the important documents like will, insurance policies, bank locker keys, cashless mediclaim cards etc. are kept so that it is not difficult to find them when they're required.

One copy of this emergency kit should be given to your spouse, and another copy may be given to a close friend.

Click Here https://links.planetwealth.in/decodedmoneyresources to download your Money Emeregncy kit template.

#26 Invest in your Career

Today, we live in a knowledge economy. We get paid not because of anything else but the knowledge, attitude and skills we bring to the table as employees in whichever company we work in. Especially in dynamic fields like Information Technology and professional services like Medical, Architecture, Accountancy, Law etc. even some months of being out of touch with latest developments can put a professional seriously on the back foot. Also, remember that our earnings in the long term are nearly directly proportional to the value and skills we contribute to our workplaces.

So, as fresh graduates into our first jobs, one is quite keen to learn & pick up new things but as one moves up the ladder & on a personal level, there are new responsibilities like getting married, kids etc., investment of quality time in the field of specialization comes down drastically & this is where the redundancy and comfort zone sets in.

Today, organisations are getting more and more aware of how their growth is a sum total of growth of the knowledge capital in their people & are creating new ways to incentivise learning – by way of sponsoring courses, inhouse training etc. Even continuous learning now forms one of the Key Performance Indicator (KPI).

Also, be on the lookout of a possibility if your employer can structure your salary in a way that some of the taxable component becomes tax free by way of reimbursement of bills for study programmes/ books however note that you'll have to submit actual bills to get the tax benefits.

Know that an investment in knowledge will pay you the best return. So set aside an annual budget and also some time for upgrading yourself in your area of specialization and other soft skills. Don't depend just on your employer for this and make sure you never become redundant in your chosen field.

I have got separate training on how to get the promotion you want. If you are interested, please click here to register your interest.

#27 Take care of your Physical Health

Isn't it illogical that people first spend all their health to gain wealth, and then spend all their wealth to gain back their health? We all can agree that our environment, food & living habits are far substandard as compared to what our earlier generations had, which actually should force us to make that much more effort to maintain it at an optimum level.

Also, bad health has a direct implication in terms of loss of pay, medical costs etc implication on your financial life. Even it's said that considering the spiralling medical inflation, the best health insurance is to take care of one's health. So, for your financial as well as over all well being, it is important to pay attention and invest quality time in taking care of your physical, mental as well as emotional health.

Some simple steps one can take in this direction are as follows:

Observe your routine – see if there is a near equal balance between work, sleep and family time. If it's highly skewed towards work, try making amends.

Watch your diet and ensure it is not at odd times, and contains balanced nutrition

Watch your sleep patterns – lack of sleep can cause severe health disorders & loss of productivity

Make it a priority to exercise, do some yoga and breathing practices in the morning. It's said that 45 minutes to one hour of brisk walk a day itself reduces the risk of diabetes and heart diseases in a big way. Yoga increases body's agility and builds immune system. Breathing practices calm the mind.

Health is Wealth has been an adage since ages. A good health is important to enjoy all the hard work you do to earn money and all the money you have accumulated over the years. Health is equally important to keep growing in your career and keep increasing your income levels.

#28 Teach your Children about Money

If you're a parent, you'll agree that children closely mimic the behaviour of parents. And it goes the same in financial matters too. So, first job for parents is to be responsible in terms of money and lead by example.

Secondly, since unfortunately our educational system does not formally teach children how they can manage money, it is imperative on the parents to consciously make efforts to educate children on money matters.

For a small 2 year old child, there will be queries or curiosity on the rupee notes, coins,etc. As a kid grows up, he'll need to be taught how to manage the money one has, why one should not borrow unnecessarily, take a kid to the bank, tell how a bank account work, how to withdraw and deposit the money etc.

This involvement of kids will raise their selfesteem in terms of handling money and will form the foundation for a better financial life for them once they start earning & managing their own money.

How to teach your Kids Personal Finance

Many parents want to equip their children with the skills they need to succeed in their financial life. Financial literacy is an important factor in helping children make sound decisions about their finances and can be a great way to teach them how to become financially independent. Teaching children financial literacy can be a daunting task for parents, but it does not have to be. With the right guidance and knowledge, parents can ensure their children have the financial literacy skills they need. We will discuss the importance of financial literacy and provide tips on how parents can teach their children sound financial practices. We will look at the basics of financial literacy, including budgeting, saving, and investing, and how to apply these concepts to everyday life. We will also discuss the various resources available to help parents teach their children financial literacy. Finally, we will provide practical tools that parents can use to help their children become more financially literate.

1. Showing the importance of money

The most important concept to teach your children about financial literacy is the importance of money. Show them the value of a dollar and discuss how it takes hard work to earn money and that it can be used to buy things. Point out the difference between wants and needs and help them understand why it is important to save money for the future. By demonstrating the importance of money, you can help your children to appreciate its value and understand the principles of financial literacy.

2. Setting a budget and showing them how to stick to it

Setting a budget and showing your children how to stick to it is an important part of teaching them financial literacy. You can help them by first having them list out all of their expenses, including allowance and any money they may receive from other sources. By having them list out their expenses, they will have a better understanding of where their money is going and how much they have to work with. Once a budget is made, you can help them keep track of it by using budgeting apps or a spreadsheet. Teaching them to stick to the budget is also important, so make sure to talk to them about the consequences of overspending and explain why it's important to stay within their budget.

3. Teaching the differences between needs and wants

One of the fundamentals of teaching financial literacy to children is to help them understand the difference between needs and wants. Explain to them that needs are essential items that are necessary to survive, like food, shelter, and clothing. Wants, on the other hand, are items that are not necessary to survive but can be nice to have, like a new toy or a special treat. Teaching children the difference between needs and wants is the first step in helping them develop good money habits.

4. Introducing the concept of saving

As soon as your children are old enough to understand the value of money, you should introduce the concept of saving. Explain to them that when they save money, it will help them to buy the things they want in the future, and that saving is an important part of being financially responsible. Show them how to save money in a piggy bank and encourage them to save some of any money they receive. You can also show them how to open a savings account and help them to understand how interest works. Teaching your children the benefits of saving from an early age will help them develop good financial habits.

5. Teaching them the basics of investing

Once your children have a basic understanding of the importance of saving and budgeting, it's time to introduce them to the basics of investing. Investing can be a great way to grow your money and is an essential part of building long-term wealth. You can start by explaining the different types of investments, such as stocks, bonds, mutual funds, and ETFs, and the differences in risk and return associated with each of them. Then, show them how to open a brokerage account and how to research potential investments. Finally, explain the importance of diversification and why it's important to spread out investments across different asset classes. This will help them understand the importance of investing for the long-term and build a better understanding of how their money can work for them.

6. Showing them how to use a credit card responsibly

Teaching your children how to use a credit card responsibly is an important part of financial literacy. First and foremost, it's important to explain to your children the purpose of a credit card, and the potential benefits and drawbacks of using a credit card. Discuss with them the importance of using their credit card responsibly and paying off the balance in full each month. Show them how to use their credit card to build their credit and to make purchases in a responsible manner. Make sure they understand the difference between a debit card and a credit card, and the consequences of not using a credit card responsibly. Finally, set an example by using your own credit card responsibly and explain to your children why you are doing so.

7. Explaining how to balance a checkbook

Learning how to balance a checkbook is a key skill to have when it comes to managing money. To begin, make sure your child has a clear understanding of the basic terminology and concepts related to a checking account, such as deposits, withdrawals, and checking account statements. Once they have a general understanding, you can start teaching them how to balance their account. You can start by having them write down the beginning balance in the check register, and then show them how to add deposits and subtract withdrawals. Have them practice balancing their checkbook by reconciling the transactions with the monthly statement. Make sure that they understand the importance of double-checking the figures and adding up the total balance with the monthly statement to ensure accuracy.

8. Understanding taxes and how to file them

Teaching your children about taxes is an important part of financial literacy. Showing them how to properly file their taxes can help them understand the importance of paying taxes and the implications of not paying them. Start by teaching them the basics of filing taxes, including what income they need to report, how to calculate their deductions, and the different types of taxes they may need to pay. Explain the importance of keeping records of their income and expenses, as well as any tax credits or deductions they are eligible for. Be sure to discuss the consequences of not filing or not paying taxes on time, as well as the potential tax liabilities they may face in their future.

In conclusion, teaching your children financial literacy is an important part of preparing them for their future. It teaches them valuable budgeting and money-managing skills, and helps them make smart decisions with their finances. It's never too early to start teaching your children financial literacy, so start introducing the concepts now and help them grow into financially responsible adults.

#29 Do Charity & if Possible Get Involved

It is said in our ancient scriptures that charity brings abundance and purifies wealth.

So, almost all religions of the world stress on setting aside some amount of one's earnings for noble causes. Apart from creating a better world, it gives a great sense of satisfaction and merit to the donor to have contributed towards betterment of the society in some way.

All of us have somewhere an altruistic desire to contribute for well being of our community, but in absence of a planned and structured process to do so, it almost never materialises till one day it's too late, and then regret takes over. Also, don't just think that only the very rich and wealthy should donate. No, everyone can and should make an attempt to donate as per his/her financial capacity.

There are NGOs like Child Relief and You & Helpage India working relentlessly for the betterment of children & senior citizens. Asides, there are payroll giving programs like GiveIndia through which you can give a standing instruction to debit a certain amount of money every month to a certified NGO of your choice.

When we talk about charity, there are many people who are willing to contribute in monetary terms, but a transformation at the ground level needs passionate and committed volunteers. You can and must go one step ahead to volunteer in whichever way you feel comfortable. Almost every NGO website has a page for volunteering opportunities. There are websites such as iVolunteer that aggregate volunteer opportunities across NGOs for you to choose from.

#30 Get a Personalized Financial Plan Done for Your Family

A planned financial life means less worry, more discipline and a very high chance of achieving the financial goals that you work for, day in and day out. The best way to plan your finances is to get a personalized financial plan. While making a personalized financial plan, the planner will look at your financial situation and goals holistically, and create tailormade solutions that are specifically meant for you, given your situation and needs.

When we speak of holistic financial planning, it means a financial planner reviews from all angles – your insurance preparedness, risk profiling, financial goals, investment planning, tax planning, succession planning etc. The recommendations that arise as a result of the planning exercise thus add a lot of value and and gives you clarity on the current scenario and way forward.

Also, a financial planner prepares a clear action plan for you to implement, along with timelines. Further to this, there is a periodic plan progress tracking to see if you are on track with your actions.

If you want to create a financial plan yourself, click here to buy an excel based financial planning software.

If you wish a professional financial planner to help you, please book 1-hour free consultancy call by clicking here : https://bookme.planetwealth.in/1-hour-free-consultancy-call.

If you want an online coaching programme on how to become your own financial planner, click here https://coaching.planetwealth.in/ to enrol for the same.

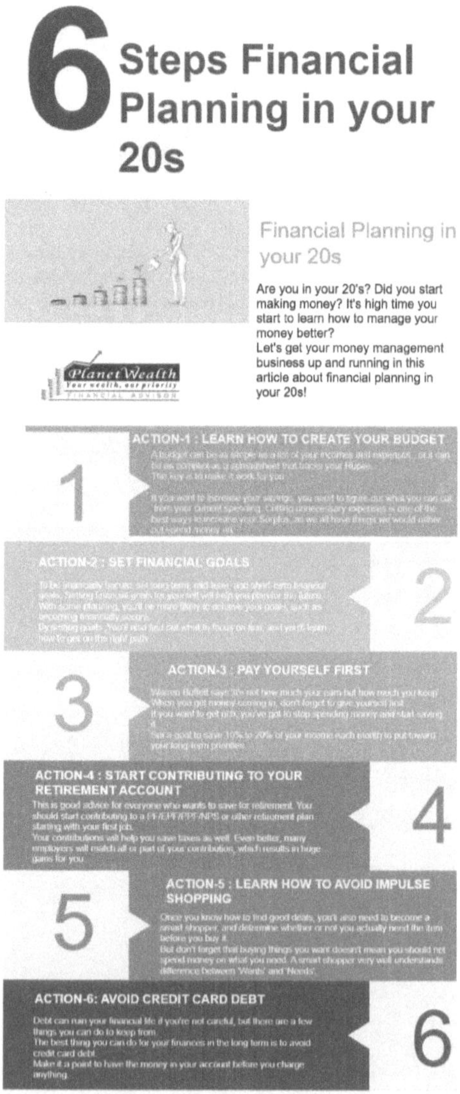

6 Steps Financial Planning in your 20s

Financial Planning in your 20s

Are you in your 20's? Did you start making money? It's high time you start to learn how to manage your money better?
Let's get your money management business up and running in this article about financial planning in your 20s!

ACTION-1 : LEARN HOW TO CREATE YOUR BUDGET

A budget can be as simple as a list of your incomes and expenses, or it can be as complex as a spreadsheet that traces your Rupee. The key is to make it work for you.

If you want to increase your savings, you need to figure out what you can cut from your current spending. Cutting unnecessary expenses is one of the best ways to increase your Surplus, as we all have things we would rather not spend money on.

ACTION-2 : SET FINANCIAL GOALS

To be financially focused, set long-term, mid-term, and short-term financial goals. Setting financial goals for yourself will help you picture your future. With some planning, you'd be more likely to achieve your goals, such as becoming financially secure.
By setting goals, you'll also find out what to focus on first, and you'll learn how to get on the right path.

ACTION-3 : PAY YOURSELF FIRST

Warren Buffett says 'It's not how much your earn but how much you keep'. When you get money coming in, don't forget to give yourself first. If you want to get rich, you've got to stop spending money and start saving it.
Set a goal to save 10% to 20% of your income each month to put toward your long-term priorities.

ACTION-4 : START CONTRIBUTING TO YOUR RETIREMENT ACCOUNT

This is good advice for everyone who wants to save for retirement. You should start contributing to a PF/EPF/PPF/NPS or other retirement plan starting with your first job.
Your contributions will help you save taxes as well. Even better, many employers will match all or part of your contribution, which results in huge gains for you.

ACTION-5 : LEARN HOW TO AVOID IMPULSE SHOPPING

Once you know how to find good deals, you'll also need to become a smart shopper, and determine whether or not you actually need the item before you buy it.
But don't forget that buying things you want doesn't mean you should not spend money on what you need. A smart shopper very well understands difference between 'Wants' and 'Needs'.

ACTION-6: AVOID CREDIT CARD DEBT

Debt can ruin your financial life if you're not careful, but there are a few things you can do to keep from.
The best thing you can do for your finances in the long term is to avoid credit card debt.
Make it a point to have the money in your account before you charge anything.

5 financial vows to take in your 30s

financial vows to take
in your 30s

once we start working, post our education, we often are not able to distinguish between our needs and desires even though there is no harm in that – at least, till a certain age. Thus, it is important to fulfil our overlapping needs and desires at the outset itself as we step into the world of financial freedom along with the ability to earn and chose our lifestyle. What's the point of life if we can't live it up to our heart's content?

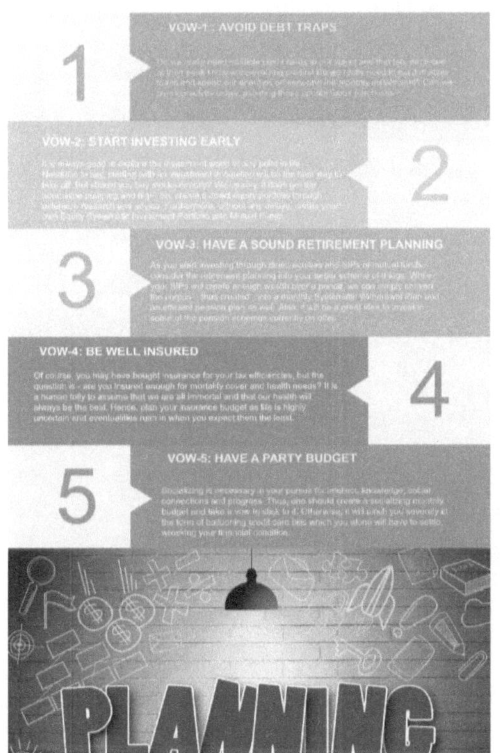

6 Steps of Financial Planning in Your 40s

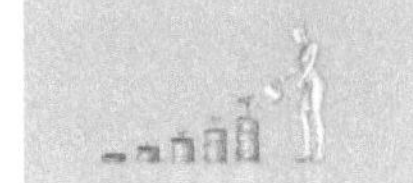

Financial Planning in your 40s

Your 40s are filled with a ton of challenges, opportunities, and big financial decisions. "Winging it" isn't an option.
There's a lot to consider for building your own financial planning, and if you're serious about becoming financially free, you'll need to understand the factors involved.

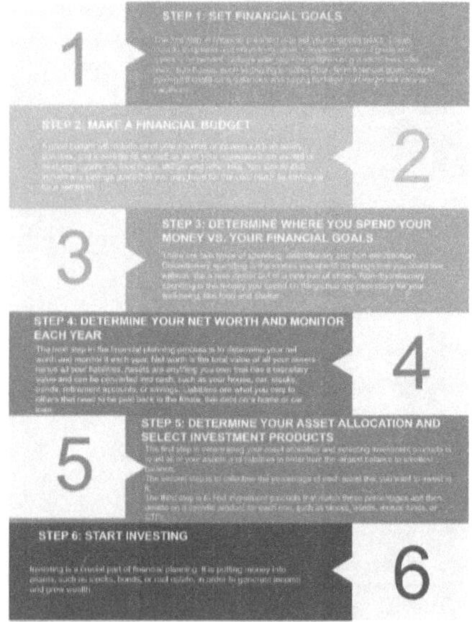

CASE STUDIES

Are You Making Mistake of Relying on Investments made in Insurance Policies for Children Education and Retirement?

r. Pandya (Name Changed to protect privacy) a senior accountant in a leading corporate who attended my Financial Literacy Seminar in his company and approached me for his financial health checkup. On examining his investments and insurances, I found his entire investments into various Moneyback and endowment Insurance Plans yielding apprx 5-6% returns per annum.

During health checkup, while interacting with him, I found he was investing 30-40% of his Salary every year for a greater period of his working life. That was by no means a less savings. After mapping his investments to his financial goals of Children Education, Marriage and Retirement, he was falling short of required corpus. Obviously his real returns after inflation were negative.

While Probing further he revealed that his brother in law was insurance agent and sold him various policies during Financial Year end and he bought the same with understanding and expecting triple advantage of saving tax along with investments for future goals and Insurance.

But in reality he was not having adequate insurance as per his Human Life Value Calculations (A calculation to determined precise insurance requirement) and his

The "M" at the start of the first body paragraph is a large drop cap.

investments were also not generating enough corpus to fulfill his requirements. He was losing on both fronts.

The reason for above situation was he bought money back/endowment investment policies where in a larger portion of the premium paid goes towards Fixed return investments by Insurance provider which generally yield returns of 5 to 6% (less than past 20 years average government inflation of 7.5% and Lifestyle inflation of 10-12%) and small part of premium goes towards mortality charges (charged by Insurance company to provide life cover in case of death) and since this charge is low, insurance cover are also low.

Its not the story of Mr. Pandya alone, a greater numbers of Investors are Mixing Investing with Insurance and continue to loose on both the requirements.

This happens because of lack of Personal Finance Literacy and Mis Selling being done by Insurance Agents who prefers to sell Moneyback/Endowment Plan as against pure term insurance plan keeping higher Commissions earnings in moneyback/endowment plans in mind.

The best way to save from such thing to happen in your life ;

Never mix Insurance and Investments.

Consult a Fee Base Financial Advisor to get your risk profiling done and do proper asset allocation based on your risk profile.

Also consult fee based financial Advisor to get your very own personal Financial Plan Prepared.

Invest in a diversified portfolio consisting of Fixed Returns and Market Returns asset classes that help you generate good tax efficient returns that help you achieve required corpus for your future goals and retirement.

Buy a term insurance plan before starting an investments plan

The reason why I have advised to consult a fees based advisor as he do not earn from commissions of selling investments product to you so he would never recommend product keeping his higher commissions earnings in mind, hence you will receive conflict free advise which in turn will protect you from any wrong/ miss selling.

I have prepared a Protection Plan , Investment Plan and retirement Plan for Mr. Pandya after administering a risk profile and preparing an asset allocation strategy for him

Now he is on his way to achieve his financial goals and worry free retirement.

So to sum up, never mix up investment and insurance as it will lead you to loose in both your requirments. Even Market linked insurance policies , known as ULIPs, also suffers from huge expenses being deducted upfront. ULIPs expense ratios are as high as 10-12% and are front loaded , means if you pay Rs. 100 premium only 88% would go for investments resulting in poor returns in initial 5 years. It is better to buy term insurance and Invest in Equity based Mutual Fund as Expense ratio for Mutual Fund has upper limit set by SEBI at maximum 2.5% and it is charged back loaded, means if you invest Rs. 100/- entire 100 would go to market and charges are deducted after a year after generating returns for you. Never miss a chance to improve your financial literacy to atleast save from mis selling happening to you. Better to consult a fees based financial Advisor to receive conflict free advise.

Are you Property/Asset Rich – Cash Poor ?

During my interaction with Investors and Clients, I keep on coming across cases where investors are Crorepati (From Net worth Point of view) but have taken personal loan @ 15-18% to finance their Financial Goals and ongoing expenses and that too with high paying government Jobs.

Being asset rich and cash poor is a problem that usually centres around property – the family home, a farm, an investment property portfolio – or a business. For young people buying their first home, the balancing act is to buy a home that is comfortable enough to live in, but not so expensive that Housing Loan repayments compromise lifestyle or the ability to reduce debt quickly.

Let me share an example of an investor ;

Income From Salaries = > 12 Lakh per annum

Real Estate Investments : Rs. 3, 65,00,000

PF : Rs. 14,00,000

Other Financial Assets : Rs. 7,00,000

Personal Loan : Rs. 5,00,000

Are They Doing Well Financially?

On paper, it would appear that this Investor should be fairing very comfortably with their 3.81 crore assets. But is that really true? Let us take a closer look.

About 90% of their net worth lies within the Real Estate that they own. Being Real Estate , it would be difficult for them to monetise this "asset".

As for the money in their PF accounts, they would need to wait until the age of 60 before they can start turning this asset into cash payout. In the meantime however, the family would need to work to ensure they have money to meet their financial goals and responsibilities such as children Education and Marriage, in spite of their net worth of more than 3 crores

This simple illustration shows why it is important to be investing today on Relatively Liquid Investments. By doing so, you are able to build a sideline income that supplements your own salary from employment.

The root cause of this Real Estate Rich – Cash Poor situation is positive experience of the Family from real Estate investments. Majority Indians share this positive experience such as Parent Bough Residence at X and the Market Value of the same is now Multiple of X. So keeping this experience in mind investors consider real estate as Safe and High Return Investments. Many are also lured by Rental incomes as well.

Another reason was informal (Black Money) economy of India uptill now so money earned from informal sources can be parked in Real Estate only.

What Investor Should do to save from such situation ?

Post De-monetisation and implementation of RERA, things have changed. India is transforming from Fixed Asset Investment such as real Estate and Gold to Financial Assets such as Mutual Fund.

So all Investor should now Balance their portfolio after considering Return and Liquidity requirements. Pls note that rental income from Residential policy in India are hardly 2-3% and for commercial property its hardly 4-6% so it doesn't cater to cash requirement of Investor.

The best solution to save from such Property Rich-Cash Poor Situation is to judiciously Plan your Asset Allocation by keeping Risk-returns and Liquidity Requirements.

How Investments Habits/ Experience inherited from Previous Generation are hurting Wealth Creation Process of New Generation?

I have observed that many of new generation Investors are following parents and grandparents while Making Investment. For E.g Investing into Bank FDs OR Investing into Various Small Savings and Post Office Schemes. When asked why, answer would be- this is how it is being done and/or they are safe.

Now, What is Safety while Investing? Infact why one is investing in the first place?

Investment is done to accumulate corpus for future major financial expenses such as Children Education or Marriage. When a family/individuals invest, she is sacrificing present Money for the betterment of tomorrow. Means utmost objective of investments is the investor should be able to meet future financial requirements. So the biggest risk an investor faces is not being able to meet future financial requirements fully or partially despite of sacrificing present.

Bank FD, Small Savings Schemes's biggest risk is that they are not giving inflation beating returns. Means by investing into such instruments investors face the risk of not accumulating sufficient corpus required to undertake major financial Expenses such as Children Marriage. Hence despite of investing by sacrificing present for the future they face shortfall in their corpus.

So another facet of risk is not being able to accumulate required corpus despite of sacrificing present Money for the future.

Now gone are the days when, our parents and grandparents from whom you have inherited/learned investment habits of investing into Bank FDs/Small Savings Schemes, were giving 12% returns and also doubling money into 5-6 years. Our parents were earning enough returns to beat inflation and grow investments to meet future financial goals. Secondly Education was largely government funded which now has become largely self-funded.

So it would not be a wise thing to follow what has been practiced by our parents and grand parents as investments and economic environment during their time were quite different than the present.

Time has changed so your investments have to be changed.

In the current scenario last 20 years average Government inflation was 7-7.5%. And if we consider Lifestyle Inflation it should be in the range of 10-12% depending on your life style.

Lets understand life style inflation with the example of movie, during the days of single screen theatre, a movie ticket was costing Rs. 40-80 and popcorn was costing Rs.10-20 and now in the age of multiplexes movie tickets are in the range of Rs. 200 to 400 and popcorn Rs. 60-100. So this inflation is not covered in government inflation but we have neither stopped going to cinemas nor even reduced frequency.

So your investment portfolio (combination of Investment Instruments such as Mutual Funds, PPF, Bank FD(if at all required) etc.) should generate at the minimum 10-12% to beat inflation and in order to grow should generate 12-14% returns over a period of time.

12-14% returns are not at all possible by investing into Bank FDs/Post Office Small Savings Schemes or PPF etc. If you wish your portfolio to not only beat inflation but grow beyond inflation, you have to come out of Investment habits inherited from your parents/Grand Parents other wise you are running serious risk of not able to meet your future financial goals even though the said investments are considered to be less risky.

The best way to start your investment journey is to first ascertain your risk profile, Investments Goals and Objectives, Tax and other Constraints and than decide strategic Asset Allocation before starting investing. Once you have decide asset allocation you may decide which investments instrument is to be used based on your financial goals. If you are not qualified to do all this things you can hire as SEBI registered Fees Only Investment advisor who should be able to help you not only to start your investment journey but shall also guide you throughout your life.

So do not become victim of inherited habits/ Experiences of your parents as situation back then were quite different than the present environment.

How I helped Client having Portfolio Lacking Diversification

As part of series of Case Studies of Clients (Names Have been changed) ;

I am sharing a case of a client whose portfolio was anything but diversified. And this wasn't his only problem. To make matters worse, he seemed to have contravened every basic tenet of wealth planning, making his portfolio an ideal candidate for a makeover.

The facts of the case:

- Mr. Sonpal is 41 years of age, and his wife Malati are both earning members.
- His sons are, Keval- aged 9 and Amul- Aged -4 respectively
- He is employed with a multinational corporation, and his salary income more than makes up for his expenses i.e. the monthly cash inflows outweigh outflows

Mr. Sonpal investments/financials are as follows:

He has invested in 3 properties (including the one in which he resides), which account for 68.5% of his assets

Traditional Insurance Policies, Bank FD and Debt investments account for 31% of assets

The balance (1%) is held in cash/savings bank accounts

He has opted for 2 child ULIPs (unit linked insurance plans), the total annual premium for which is Rs. 130,000

On the liabilities front, he has an outstanding home loan and also a loan against his mutual fund investment

As can be seen, property i.e. real estate as an asset class accounts for a disproportionately high portion of the asset portfolio. Furthermore, all the properties are in the same city, depriving the client of any diversification opportunity. While it is important to have property in one's portfolio, it certainly should not account for such a high proportion. Also given that property as an asset class tends to be rather illiquid (a distress sale when liquidity needs are urgent could lead to a loss-making proposition), only accentuates the unenviable situation. A downturn in property prices could spell disaster for the client.

The remedy for this situation lies in introducing other assets like equities into the portfolio and thereby converting the portfolio into a more balanced one. Studies have shown that equities as an asset class (if invested smartly) can outperform others like real estate, gold and fixed income instruments over longer time frames. Considering that the client needs (planning for retirement and providing for children's education) are long-term in nature, the presence of a higher equity component should be treated as vital.

The present solution should be to put on hold any plans to buy more property. It is always recommended that each individual should be invested in property to the extent that it can provide for inheritance. With 3 properties, the client has adequately taken care of that.

The surplus cash inflows should now be utilized to beef up the portfolio equity component. But the same needs to be done in a planned manner. Sadly, the client has not even set himself any concrete objective in terms of planning for retirement or providing for children education. In other words, it is yet another case of investing randomly without setting any objectives. To complicate matters, the client has erred investing in bank

FD and Traditional Policies yielding negative real rate of returns.

The solution – set objectives (in monetary terms) and then invests in well managed equity funds in a disciplined manner for achieving the same. This well help on various levels.

First, the enhanced equity component will ensure that the portfolio become well-diversified across asset classes.

Second, it will make the equity investments diversified across multiple schemes. Finally, it will aid in gainfully utilizing the surplus monies.

The liability side could do with some rework as well. While the home loan can aid in tax-planning (interest and principal repayments qualify for deduction from gross total income), we are not quite convinced about the loan against mutual fund investment. The client is sufficiently does not need to shoulder the burden of a redundant loan repayment. He would be better off paying off the loan at the earliest.

The client financial status and condition make rather interesting reading. On the surface, we have an individual, whose income streams more than make up for his expenses, whose asset portfolio seems rather well-stocked. In other words, it is a seemingly picture perfect situation. But scratch the surface, and a radically different picture emerges.

The investments are lop-sided in favour of a single asset class (i. e. property). Despite the needs being long-term in nature, the client is virtually unprepared to meet those needs; in fact, he hasn't even quantified his needs – which should be the starting point for the exercise. He doesn't have an adequate insurance cover and has in his books avoidance liabilities.

The case only underscores the difference between having finances and being financially sound. And missing out on the latter could well mean that one is headed for a financial disaster.

HOW I HELPED MY CLIENT : THE IMPORATANCE OF STARTING EARLY

The client, Mr. Mehta is a 55-Yr old individual, employed with a private sector enterprise. His family comprises of his wife (a homemaker) and a son. Mr. Mehta earns an annual salary of Rs. 10, 00,000; broadly speaking, his annual expenses amount to Rs. 500,000 (Rs. 350,000 towards household expenses and Rs. 150,000 towards travelling/holidays).

When I met Mr. Mehta, he expressed his desire to retire in 5 years. Also, he wanted to provide for his son 2 – Yr MBA programme, 7 years down the line. The outlay for the same would be around Rs. 500000 per annum (pa). Finally, with more time on hand, he wanted to travel more frequently, implying additional expenses, around Rs. 250,000 pa.

Mr. Mehta holds an investment portfolio which at present is worth nearly Rs. 40, 00,000. The same is lop-sided in favour of assured return schemes like bonds, fixed deposits and small savings schemes, several of which rank poorly on the liquidity front. Only a minor portion of the portfolio is allocated to equities and mutual funds. Also, he has bought an endowment plan that will offer him a maturity value of Rs. 10, 00,000 (after taking into account the bonus).

What the numbers indicate: to begin with, I computed the future value (as on the retirement date) of Mr. Mehta present investment portfolio. Assuming an average growth rate of 8% pa, it amounted to a maturity value of around Rs. 5,877,000. Then I computed the post-retirement expenses (household expenses, travel costs and the corpus required for the son's education). After factoring in inflation and assuming a life expectancy of 75 year Rs. And the numbers proved to be eye-openers, to say the least. Over a 5-Yr period, Mr. Mehta needs to accumulate a retirement kitty of approximately Rs. 4,900,000, over and above his existing investments to meet all the aforementioned expenses. This is turn, amounts to making investment of Rs. 61,000 or an annual investment of a Rs. 772,000 (assuming a 12% CAGR).

Given how Mr. Mehta finances are placed at present, it would not be possible for him to save and invest the required monies. Even if he were to invest his entire savings from now until retirement (i. e. around Rs. 500,000 pa), the target seems unachievable.

Solution

Mr. Mehta finds himself in a rather unenviable situation. He faces the prospect of having to compromise on his lifestyle. For instance, post-retirement, he can consider holidaying less frequently and/or curtailing his household expenses. Mr. Mehta can consider not retiring at the end of 5 years, given that he is employed with a private sector enterprise. Or maybe post-retirement, he can think of working as a consultant in order to supplement his finances. Finally, he can explore the possibility of asking his son to avail of an education loan to finance his higher education.

Simply put, barring the possibility of receiving an unexpected windfall, Mr. Mehta's dreams of a picture-perfect retirement has certainly gone awry.

As I mentioned earlier, I wanted to use this case to highlight the downside of not starting the retirement planning process early. On the surface, Mr. Mehta earning a handsome salary and leading a comfortable lifestyle might give the impression of all being in order. But as is often the case, the habit of making investments in a sporadic manner and leaving too much for later, does spell trouble.

In conclusion, providing for retirement need not be a difficult task. All one needs to do is plan methodically and have sufficient time on hand. And the implications of not doing so should motivate one to get started in earnest, at the earliest.

CASE STUDY: WEALTH PLANNING FOR RETIREES

This is the case of an individual who was 65 years of age, and had already retired and wanted to plan for cash flows for the rest of his life...

So, what was his main wealth planning objective? – To invest his corpus of Rs. 1.50 crore, so as to meet his expenses of Rs. 1 lakh per month (i.e. Rs. 12 lakh per annum) on an ongoing basis. Another noteworthy point was he had a secondary corpus of Rs. 50 lakh which he preferred not to use for the plan.

Details were as follows:

Name:	Mr. Jayesh Patel
Status:	NRI
Life Stage:	Retired
Investible Corpus:	Rs. 1.50 crore
Risk Appetite:	No risk –no capital loss is acceptable.
Goal:	Assured monthly income of Rs. 1 lakh, starting immediately, going on for life.
Life Expectancy:	85 years

Reason No. 1: The required return was not achievable in present times, by taking shelter under "safe debt investments" alone.

In order to earn assured income of Rs. 12 lakhs p.a. (post tax) from a corpus of Rs. 1.50 crore, assuming

30% tax, the pretax income required is approximately Rs. 17 lakhs per annum. The rate of return needed to earn this income is close to 11.50% p.a., which is currently unachievable, especially if corporate deposits are also not to be considered. Moreover, taking into account his low appetite for risk and guarantee for monthly income, exposing him to an equity allocation wasn't the right option.

So, what were the available investment Options in "safe debt instrument":

Small Saving Schemes: When an individual looks safety and guaranteed return, small savings are the first that any wealth manager looks at. However, noting that he was an NRI, this option too was not available to do his planning. Small savings schemes such as PPf, Post Office Monthly Income Schemes, and Senior Citizen Saving Scheme – are off-limits for NRIs.

Bank/Corporate FDs: Yes, we can explore this option too, noting that the required rate of return is 11.50% p.a. But, presently as bank FDs are offering only between 8.00% and 8.50 % for the 1-2 year tenure for senior citizens, this option too was ruled out.

Immediate Annuity Pension Schemes: Taking into account that he's a retired individual, we evaluated this option too. But this again did not meet the expectations of 11.50% rate of return, as the rate of return offered on such products are 7.50% per annum- again pretax.

These are schemes wherein the investor invests his money as a lump sum / regular premium today and starts receiving premium payment immediately, going on far a specified term period or for life, as opted.

So, clearly, from a rate of return point of view, we are in a fix. And there was yet another reason why the corpus would not have been enough.

Reason No. 2: Inflation

Mr. Jayesh Patel needs Rs. 1 lakh per month (i.e. Rs. 12 lakhs p.a.) post tax today. That's 11.50% return pretax. But taking 7% average inflation rate, he will need more income, from the same principal (Rs. 1.50 crore), to meet the same lifestyle expenses. Here's a snapshot:

	Monthly income(Post tax) in Rs	Annual income(Post tax) in Rs	Annual income(Post tax) in Rs	Pretax rate of return
Income required today	1,00,000	12,00,000	17,15,000	11.50%
Income required in 5 years	1,40,000	16,80,000	24,00,000	16.00%
Income required in 10 years	1,96,000	23,50,000	33,60,000	22.40%
Income required in 5 years	2,76,000	33,12,000	47,32,000	31.50%

*Figures are approximate

And all the while "his investible corpus remains the same i.e. Rs. 1.50 crore. So, given the facts, in present times the solution was simple and realistic.

We said at current rates of interest and given risk appetite and required corpus – the goals is not achievable, and the only way out was adjust the goal or increase the available corpus.

The solution: we can guide Mr. Jayesh Patel through what he needs to do in order to make the most of his available corpus while making sure he is within his comfort zone on the risk appetite front. The wealth manager can provide him with a cash flow for his whole life, showing how his income would be generated, and how his expenses would grow with inflation.

With a corpus of Rs. 2 crore, and taking no risk on his capital, Mr. Jayesh Patel is able to achieve monthly income Rs. 72,000 approximately, growing yearly to meet inflation.

Key Takeaways

As wealth manager I am to provide an investor with a true and unbiased wealth plan, thus not just helping him achieve his financial goals, but are ensuring that he is financially healthy, by taking only optimal risk to achieve the required rate of return.

WEALTH PLANNING FOR SINGLE WOMEN

When it comes to making investment decisions, women tend to shift this responsibility on their close family member. While trusting one's close family members is not wrong; completely depending on them can lead to trouble when one is left alone. The reasons could be an eventuality in the family or a separation from spouse.

Separation leads not only to emotional distress but can also make women financially handicapped, especially when they are not working or the spouse was managing the finances. Therefore, to secure one's life financially, it is important for women to have a wealth plan.

Facts of the case

Ms. Bimla Pathak is 32 years old and is working as a Deputy Managar with a Bank and drawing a post-tax salary of Rs. 30,000 per month (p.m.).

She has a 5 years old son.

She had taken car loan for 5 years @ 12%; the EMI for this comes to Rs 8,500.

She had taken a joint home loan for 2BHK apartment with her ex-husband for 20 years; the total EMI for this comes to Rs. 25,000.

Her total monthly expenses are Rs 24,500 p.m.

Instruments	Corpus(Rs)
Public Provident Fund (PPF)*	50,000
Fixed Deposites (FD)*	120,000
Cash	100,000
Gold jewellery	100,000
Total Assets	370,000

Current Portfolio

*PPf will mature after 11 years and FD will mature after 5 years

Observations

Ms. Pathak cannot maintain the same lifestyle given her current circumstances.

Her investments were in conventional fixed income instruments with no exposure to equity.

Her loans i.e. car loan EMIs and home loan EMIs took away more than 50% of her salary.

Before separation, she was dependent on her husband for her personal expenses.

She was not similar with different investment avenues.

The course of action

After conducting several rounds of discussion with Ms. Bimla Pathak, the wealth manager identified her immediate and long-term was to buy a house. The other goals were buying car, saving for her child's education and her retirement.

Financial goals	Time horizon(years)	Future cost (Rs)
Buying a house	5	675,000*
Son's Education	12	3,000,000
Retirement	28	11,200,000

*comprises of down-payment (35, 00,000 x 15%) + 150,000 of stamp duty & registration

Assumptions

The manager advised her to maintain at least Rs. 100,000 in bank account to meet any contingency.

Interest income on cash is not considered as part of her monthly income.

He assumed her salary will grow by 10% p.a. and inflation will increase by 6% p.a.

The manager has not considered the impact of alimony in this case study. However, for women in similar situations that can be an additional source of income.

The current house will be either transferred in the name of her ex-husband or sold. We assumed that there was no profit generated from this transaction.

He assumes her life expectancy to be 75 years.

He has assumed return of 7 % p.s. post-tax on investment in fixed deposits and equity.

Solution

Cut down expenses: the manager started Ms. Pathak's wealth planning by projecting her monthly cash flows by getting the break-up of income, expenses and savings. The table below shows that her monthly expenses were more than 90% of her salary, which led to negligible savings. Hence the first advise was to stop spending liberally on things that were secondary for her day-to-day operations. To name a few, spending on movies, dinner, vacations, shopping are some of the expenses that she was advised to cut down on. Spending more can lead to increase in debt and reduced savings, which in turn would delay her financial goals.

The wealth manager advised her to sell her current car and prepay the loan and defer this goal by 3 years.

Monthly Budget	Current (Rs)	Recommended (RS)
Salary	30,000	30,000
Total Expenses	24,500	18,000
(a)Household exp.	15,000	9,000
(b)Child's Education	1,000	1,000
(c)Car EMI	8,500	-
(d)House Rent	-	8,000
Total Savings(A-B)	5,500	12,000

Opt for Insurance: The most important instrument that was missing in her portfolio was insurance. Insuarance helps the insured's dependents in case of the eventuality. In this case, her 5-yr old son was the sole dependent and has at least another 15 years before which he can take care of himself financially. Hence the manager suggested her to opt for term insurance policy for cover of Rs. 50 lakhs for 20 years Rs. The annual premium for this comes to Rs. 14,000.

Next he advised her to opt for medical insurance with insurance cove of Rs. 5 lakhs. The premium for the same worked out to Rs. 5,000 per year.

Buying house: based on her income, financial commitments and ability to service the loan, the manager advised her to opt for a 1 BHK house worth Rs. 35 lakhs. She should avail of home loan for 85% of the cost. He advised her to stay in a rented apartment till the time she is able to accumulate the corpus for the down-payment and the stamp duty and registration fees. The monthly rental worked out to Rs. 8,000 p.m.

Next step was to make a plan for accumulating corpus of Rs. 675,000. The stamp duty and registration charges of Rs. 150,000 will be taken care by the fixed deposit which will mature after 5 years Rs. For the down-payment of Rs. 525.000, the manager advised her to invest Rs. 7,300 p.m. for next five years, assuming return of 7 % p.a. post-tax.

Son's education plan: Ms. Pathak wishes to send her son to engineering college after completion of junior college i.e. after 12 years Rs. The expenses for the same worked out to Rs. 30 Lakhs. The manager advised her to avail education loan same worked out to Rs. 30 lakhs. The manager advised her to avail education loan for 80% of the estimated cost. For the balance cost of Rs. 6 lakhs, he advised her to invest Rs. 2,700 p.m. for next twelve years, assuming return of 7 % p.a. post-tax.

Retirement planning: Ms. Pathak plans to retire at the age of 55 years. Given her current financial commitments, she cannot start planning for her retirement immediately. Hence, it was suggested that she start her retirement planning from the age of 43.

Her expenses post-retirement will comprise of:
Household expenses
Premium towards medical insurance
Healthcare expenses
Travelling expenses

Assuming growth of 10% p.a. in salary was expected to be Rs. 10 lakhs p.a. at age of 43. Considering her current house hold expenses and travelling /healthcare expenses; her retirement corpus worked out to Rs. 44,200 p.m. from the age of 43 years till the age of 55 years, assuming return of 7% p.a. post-tax.

Financial goals	Time horizon(years)	Future cost (Rs)	Start investment at the age of	Investment horizon (years)	Investment required per month (Rs)	CAGR(%)
Buying a house	5	675,000*	32	5	7,300	7%
Son's Education	12	3,000,000	32	12	2,700	7%
Retirement	28	11,200,000	43	13	44,200	7%

Summary of wealth plan

Asset Allocation: The risk-appetite of Ms. Bimla Pathak's moderate. Hence the wealth manager recommended asset allocation of 45% in equity and 55% in debt. As she does not have the required skill sets to invest in equity mutual funds via SIP route. For debt investments, he advised her to invest in equity directly, he advised her to invest in equity mutual funds via SIP route. For debt investments, he advised her to invest in fixed deposits and debt mutual funds. We also advised her to invest in tax efficient products like ELSS and PPF to save on taxes.

Key Takeaways: Women whether single, married or separated should carefully plan their finances. Women who find themselves similar situations should follow these steps:

Take stock of the finances

Identify key financial goals such as child's education.

Identify your risk appetite

If one cannot handle volatility in the portfolio then keep the equity allocation low. Risk-appetite of each individual is different. Hence the asset allocation will vary from person to person.

Buy Insurance

The insurance cover should depend on the monetary value of all yet-to-be fulfilled needs of the dependents plus all outstanding liabilities.

Save more, cut-down expenses

Saving is important for the success of one's financial goals. It's very important for individuals to understand that they cannot afford to maintain the same life style post-separation. As the total income reduces, so should the expenses.

Review the wealth plan

It is important to review the wealth plan with the wealth manager at regular at regular intervals. The changes in equity market, risk-appetite, goals etc. would require change in the asset allocation.

WEALTH PLANNING

Ram Krishan Murthy and Veena Murthy is a salaried couple staying in Chennai. Ram Krishan works as a programmer for an IT firm, while Veena works in the administration department of an FMCG company. The family comprises of 6 members, Ram Krishan & Veena, their 2 kinds and Ram Krishan's parents.

Financial goals	Time horizon(years)	Future cost (Rs)	Start investment at the age of	Investment horizon (years)	Investment required per month (Rs)	CAGR(%)
Buying a house	5	675,000*	32	5	7,300	7%
Son's Education	12	3,000,000	32	12	2,700	7%
Retirement	28	11,200,000	43	13	44,200	7%

Their inflows, outflows & Net worth Details are given below.

	Monthly	yearly
Inflows		
Ram Krishan	64500	774000
Veena	21000	252000
	85500	1026000
Outflows		
Household expenses	27500	330000
Life insurance	5333.33	64000
Total Outflow	32833.3	394000
Investments		
PPF	5833.3	70000
Surplus	46833.3	562000
Net Worth		
Self-Occupied home	4200000	
Savings Account	550000	
PPF(both accounts)	400000	
EPF(both accounts)	445000	
Stocks & Mutual funds	-0	
Net worth	5795000	

Veena has decided to discontinue after 1 year concentrate on her children's education. Both the kids are going to school and grandparents take the reasonability of looking after them during the day, in the absence of Ram Krishan & Veena. Ram Krishan would like to continue in the IT industry and the family's financial goals are enumerated below.

Insurance

In spite of paying an annual premium of Rs.64000, Ram Krishan is covered for a sum assured of Rs. 12 lakhs while is covered for Rs. 400000. Ram Krishan's Employer provides group floater mediclaim cover of Rs. 300000 for the family of 4, excluding the parents. Parents are not covered by any form of medical insurance.

FINANCIAL GOALS

The following are the financial goals as enumerated by Ram Krishan and Veena in present value terms.

Educational funding of Alisha – Rs. 1 lakh each year from age 17 to 10 and Rs. 3 lakhs at her of 21 years

Educational funding of Govind – Rs. 1 lakh each year from age 17 to 20 and Rs. 3 lakhs at his age of 21 years

Marriage funding of Alisha – Rs. 4 lakhs at her age of 26 years

Marriage funding of Govind at his age of 27 years

Retirement in the year 2031 when Ram Krishan turns 58 years old.

Sr. No.	Financial Goal Category:- Responsibilities	Today's cost	Approximate No. of years	Year	Inflation Adjusted Cost
1	Daughters Education'				
1.2	Required at Age 17 Years	Rs. 100,000.00	10	2021	Rs. 259,374
1.3	Required at Age 18 Years	Rs. 100,000.00	11	2022	Rs.285,312
1.4	Required at Age 19 Years	Rs. 100,000.00	12	2013	Rs.313,843
1.5	Required at Age 20 Years	Rs. 100,000.00	13	2024	Rs.345,227
1.6	Required at Age 21 Years	Rs. 300,000.00	14	2025	Rs.1,139,250
		Rs. 700,000.00			Rs. 2,343,005
2	Son's Education				
2.2	Required at age 17 years	Rs. 100,000.00	13	2024	Rs. 345,227
2.3	Required at Age 18 years	Rs. 100,000.00	14	2025	Rs. 379,750
2.4	Required at Age 19 Years	Rs. 100,000.00	15	2026	Rs. 417,725
2.5	Required at Age 20 Years	Rs. 100,000.00	16	2027	Rs.459,497
2.6	Required at Age 21 Years	Rs. 300,000.00	17	2028	Rs. 1,516,341
		Rs. 700,000.00			Rs. 3,118,540
3	Marriage of Daughter	Rs. 400,000.00	19	2029	Rs.2,446,364
4	Marriage of son	Rs. 400,000.00	22	2032	Rs. 3,256,110
5	Retirement at Age 58 years				
	Expenses Considered	Rs. 252,000.00	20	2027	Rs. 1,070,458
	Corpus Required		20		Rs.22,953,250

Assumptions
General inflation (retirement) – 7.5 %
Educational & marriage inflation – 10 %
Expected annual increase in salary – 5 %
Return on Equity & Equity mutual funds – 12%
Return on PPF - 8%
Return on EPF- 8.5 %
Retirement corpus growth 1.87 % (adjusted to inflation)

PROJECTIONS AND RECOMMEDATIONS

Contingency Fund:

The family should maintain a contingency fund Rs. 83000 9rounded off). Rs 15000to maintain as cash at home and the rest in his savings account linked with FD.

Considering Ram Krishan's parents health status and the fact that they don't have any medical cover, Rs. 300000 to be maintained in a bank FD as a backup for their unforeseen medical expenses.

The above allocation can be managed from the savings account balance

INSURANCE

Accident: Ram Krishan should take an accident policy of 25 lakhs with a TTD 9Total temporary benefit) of 7.5 lakhs. The premium will come to around Rs. 3500.

Health: Ram Krishan and Veena should take an individual cover of Rs. 5 lakhs each and Rs. 2 lakhs for their daughters, the premium for which will. be approximately Rs. 2 lakhs for their daughters, the premium for which will be approximately Rs. 15500.

Life: As per the expenses replacement method there is a shortfall of Rs. 80 lakhs of life insurance cover which should be covered by term plan for a period of 25 years at an approximate cost of Rs. 20000 p.a.

FINANCIAL GOALS

For daughters educational requirement starting from 17th to 21st year of her age, SIP in Equity Diversified

Mutual fund to be started for an amount of Rs. 6750.

For son's educational requirement starting from his 17th to 21st year a sip of Rs. 5750 to be started in a Diversified Equity mutual fund.

Daughter's Marriage requirement can be funded by starting an SIP of Rs. 3000 in a diversified MF.

Son's marriage can be funded by starting an SIP of Rs. 2500 in a Nifty Index MF.

The retirement expenses at age 58 will be Rs. 10, 70,458 per year for which a corpus of Rs. 2, 29, 53,250 is required which can sustain till the age of 85 years.

A major part of the corpus can be easily funded by PF, PPF & Gratuity benefits which will altogether fetch Rs. 1, 59, 15,000 at retirement. The shortfall of Rs. 70,38,000 can be achieved by starting an SIP of Rs. 7250 in an Index Mutual fund.

RECOMMENDED CASH FLOW

Total Inflow	85500	1026000
Outflows		
Household expenses	27500	330000
Life insurance	7000	84000
Accident & Mediclaim	1583.33	19000
PPF	5833.33	70000
SIPs	25250	30300
Total Outflow	67166.7	806000
Surplus	18333.3	220000

The surplus can be maintained in savings bank and can be used to fund the SIPs for next year when Veena won't be working.

Poor Cash Management Skills stopping retail investors from Creating Wealth

'I don't have surplus money; how can I Invest' - Majority of retail Investor I interact with during my Financial Well Being Workshops have common feedback when it comes to investing.

This is common and relates to poor cash management and budgeting skills. Poor cash Management and budgeting skills do not allow investor to save and invest which done properly help them create enough wealth as provided by their cashflows i.e income.

I have many clients earning 70k to 1 lakh per month but prior to meeting me they were hardly saving 15 to 20K per month and were happy that they are investing for their better future. During my initial meeting I conduct Financial Health Checkup and I have found that majority investors are losing opportunity to create wealth as the do not understand possibility of investments provided by proper cash flow management. I have observed following amongst such investors;

They have surplus cash but in the absence of proper budgeting, they do not realize and invest less and loose wealth creation opportunity.

Mostly investors surplus cash gets consumed as there is a saying 'if you do not direct cash, cash will have its own direction' which may not be in consistency of your life goals and requirements

Lack of Goal Based planning also prohibit them to allocate financial resources towards their priorities as most of them are not clear with their priorities. For e.g. Recently one Prospective client who during health checkup wished to buy a new home but despite both earning their current cash flow was drained by Car Loan Instalments and hence they were not able to save for home and are in conflicting situation of choosing to invest for either children's education and marriage or buying home.

Best way is to avoid this cash flow trap is to prepare a yearly budget in the beginning of the month and then decide allocation of cash according to your own priority. Investor do need to define their financial goals as it will help them to prioritize their cash flow as per their need.

I always start financial planning with cashflow and budgeting worksheet and then help investor to define and articulate their financial goals and objectives in order to maximize their wealth creation.

How to go about Creating your Personal Cash Flow Statement

To create a personal cash flow statement, does require some discipline.

Why is that? This is because for some People have never been aware where their money is flowing to.

You need to keep track of where the large part of your money is flowing to.

On a high level, you need to:

Identify different sources of income that results in a cash inflow

Identify different categories of cash outflows

Track the cash inflow and cash outflows

Calculate the cash inflow – cash outflows

If you would like to get started, you can use download personal cashflow management worksheet from

https://links.planetwealth.in/decodedmoneyresources for you to Kick Start.

You can compile one version of this for your recurring cash inflows and cash outflows on an annual basis. Some people might want to update their cash flow statement every quarterly.

In summary your proper budgeting and cashflow management skills can help you achieve wealth you wish to create as also help you achieve a balance between your present financial goals and your future financial goals and objectives ensuring your peace of mind.

WEALTH CREATION OPPORTUNITY LOST BY YOUNG INDIANS

During my career as Financial Coach, advisor and Planner, I have experienced that majority of young Executives are not recognizing and understanding " Power of Compounding" and are not starting investing in the early days of their career. It is because financial goals are far away (such as retirement etc.) in their career so they do not realise how it would be hurting if they do not start investing in early days of career. Lest understand power of compounding by following illustration ;

To create a corpus of Approx. 5 crore, you need to invest:

Image Courtesy : ET- Wealth

So by delaying Investments young Indians are losing their chance of creating enormous wealth during their career span. My experience suggest that young Indians delay investments because of following execuses ;

I have just started earning, let me enjoy my life

I don't earn enough so that I can Invest some meaningful amount

Why do I start investing at this stage when I don't have any Financial Responsibility

Lack of Financial Literacy

The best way to not to become victim of above pro-castination is to try and understand power of compounding an start using it in your favor rather than allowing it to work against you. Doing this will help you by following way ;

Being young and with no or little financial responsibility, you will be able to save more of cashflow as compared to in future with family responsibility

It will not only help you to accumulate greater wealth but also allow you to invest relatively less %age of your income when you have full family financial responsibilities thus empowering you to spend more on current than saving for future.

There will no perfect day or monthly savings which will help you to start perfect, you just need to start Investing and gradually you will be able to save and Invest you wished for.

One of my client in his early thirties got a job of Rs. 10000 per month and following my advise he staraight away started investing 5000 per month in his portfolio and if continues to invest the same amount throughout his career till his retirement, he would be able to amass greater than 3 crores. Now you can imagine the real "Power of compounding" that empowers a mere Rs. 10,000 monthlt earner can become crorepati which you would never have thought about.

To understand what could be impact of NOT starting early, I also have one client, working as sr. position in accounting department of a listed corporate, who have not started savings and investments early in life and after experiencing effect of delay approached me for retirement planning and on analyzing his financial data and preparing his retirement plan, I have to painfully educate and prepare him that he would have to work for 5 years after retirement to generate supplement income to avoid him outliving his retirement corpus generated through retirement investment plan.

So in nut shall as young indian executive, you should not spend all your salary and start an investment plan to;

1. Become Crorepati
2. Live a Financially Fulfilled and Peaceful Life

And

1. to become crorepati , you should stop giving excuses and start investing right from first salary.